FOR REFERENCE

Do Not Take From This Room

WORLD WAR II

JAPAN'S PACIFIC ONSLAUGHT

1941-1942

Volume 4

an imprint of

www.scholastic.com/librarypublishing

Published 2006 by Grolier,
an imprint of Scholastic Library Publishing
Old Sherman Turnpike
Danbury, Connecticut 06816

© 2006 The Brown Reference Group plc

Set ISBN-13: 978-0-7172-6159-8
Set ISBN-10: 0-7172-6159-X
Volume ISBN-13: 978-0-7172-6163-5
Volume ISBN-10: 0-7172-6163-8

Library of Congress Cataloging-in-Publication Data
World War II.
      v. cm.
   Includes bibliographical references and index.
   Contents: v. 1. Origins of the war -- v. 2. Europe in flames,
1939-1941 -- v. 3. The Eastern Front, 1941-1943 -- v. 4. Japan's
Pacific onslaught, 1941-1942 -- v. 5. The tide turns in the West,
1942-1943 -- v. 6. The tide turns in the Pacific, 1942-1944 -- v. 7.
The wider war -- v. 8. Europe, 1944-1945 -- v. 9. Victory in the
Pacific, 1944-1945 -v. 10. The aftermath of the war.

   ISBN-13: 978-0-7172-6159-8 (set : alk. paper)
   ISBN-10: 0-7172-6159-X (set : alk. paper)
   ISBN-13: 978-0-7172-6160-4 (v. 1 : alk. paper)
   ISBN-10: 0-7172-6160-3 (v. 1 : alk. paper)
   ISBN-13: 978-0-7172-6161-1 (v. 2 : alk. paper)
   ISBN-10: 0-7172-6161-1 (v. 2 : alk. paper)
   ISBN-13: 978-0-7172-6162-8 (v. 3 : alk. paper)
   ISBN-10: 0-7172-6162-X (v. 3 : alk. paper)
   ISBN-13: 978-0-7172-6163-5 (v. 4 : alk. paper)
   ISBN-10: 0-7172-6163-8 (v. 4 : alk. paper)
   ISBN-13: 978-0-7172-6164-2 (v. 5 : alk. paper)
   ISBN-10: 0-7172-6164-6 (v. 5 : alk. paper)
   ISBN-13: 978-0-7172-6165-9 (v. 6 : alk. paper)
   ISBN-10: 0-7172-6165-4 (v. 6 : alk. paper)
   ISBN-13: 978-0-7172-6166-6 (v. 7 : alk. paper)
   ISBN-10: 0-7172-6166-2 (v. 7 : alk. paper)
   ISBN-13: 978-0-7172-6167-3 (v. 8 : alk. paper)
   ISBN-10: 0-7172-6167-0 (v. 8 : alk. paper)
   ISBN-13: 978-0-7172-6168-0 (v. 9 : alk. paper)
   ISBN-10: 0-7172-6168-9 (v. 9 : alk. paper)
   ISBN-13: 978-0-7172-6169-7 (v. 10 : alk. paper)
   ISBN-10: 0-7172-6169-7 (v. 10 : alk. paper)

   1. World War, 1939-1945--Encyclopedias. I. Grolier (Firm) II.
Title: World War Two. III. Title: World War 2.
   D743.W6496 2006
   940.5303--dc22
                                      2006011371

For information address the publisher:
Scholastic Library Publishing
Old Sherman Turnpike,
Danbury, Connecticut 06816

Printed and bound in Singapore

Text: Chris McNab, Tony Hall, Charles Bowery

Consultant: Professor Dennis Showalter, Department of
            History, Colorado College, Colorado Springs

ABOUT THIS BOOK

World War II was the largest and most destructive war in history. Between 1939 and 1945, 100 million troops were mobilized across the world—in Europe, Africa, and West and East Asia. It was a war fought with weapons of previously unseen destructiveness, culminating in the use of two atomic bombs in Japan. As many as 60 million people may have died in the war. Most of them were civilians who died as a result of aerial bombing, starvation, disease, or persecution by brutal regimes. The biggest crime against civilians was the murder of six million of Europe's Jews by the Nazis.

This set of 10 books tells the stories of key events, individuals, and battles of this long and bitter war. It examines the roots of the conflict, which lay largely in political tensions that remained unresolved after World War I. The books cover the political, economic, social, and technological context of the fighting, and describe how noncombatants on home fronts around the world were affected by war. The final book in the set explores the repercussions of World War II, detailing the massive shift in the world's balance of power and the onset of the Cold War.

The set is full of dramatic photographs depicting the world at war, and full-color maps that show you where the action took place. There are also eyewitness accounts and feature boxes that highlight particular aspects of the conflict for closer examination. Every chapter ends with a list of cross-references to related entries so that you can follow up particular topics. At the end of each book there is a further reading list that includes Web sites, a glossary of special terms, and an index covering all 10 volumes.

FOR THE BROWN REFERENCE GROUP PLC

Project Editor:	Selina Wood
Commissioning Editors:	Emily Hill, Selina Wood
Editors:	Sylvia and David Tombesi-Walton
	Rachel Bean, Jane Edmonds
Editorial consultant:	Peter Darman
Designers:	Paul Griffin, Iain Stuart
Picture Researchers:	Andrew Webb, Becky Cox
Maps:	Mark Walker, Darren Awuah
Indexer:	Kay Ollerenshaw
Managing Editor:	Tim Cooke
Design Managers:	Sarah Williams, Lynne Ross
Production Director:	Alastair Gourlay
Editorial Director:	Lindsey Lowe

CONTENTS

THE APPROACH OF WAR

The Japanese attack on Pearl Harbor on December 7, 1941, stunned the world. In fact, the storm clouds of war had been gathering over the Pacific for two decades.

Japan had begun modernizing in 1867. Reformers overthrew the old government in the so-called Meiji Restoration. They ended centuries of international isolation. They set up a new government, and began industrial development modeled on Western lines. The Japanese also began a program of expansion. They needed resources to support their industrial growth. In the latter decades of the 19th century, Japan added numerous islands to its empire. It defeated China in the Sino-Japanese War

(1894–1895). It showed its growing military strength again with a surprise defeat of Russia in the Russo-Japanese War (1904–1905). In 1910, Japan annexed the Korean peninsula.

In World War I (1914–1918), Japan backed the Western allies. It took control of German possessions in the Pacific and China. The 1919 Treaty of Versailles confirmed Japan's gains (*see Volume 1, Chapter 1*). They included the Palau, Caroline, and Marshall islands, and part of the Marianas. Japan also kept control of Germany's former territories in northeast China, to the resentment of the Chinese.

▼ Japanese troops land at Hangchow Bay in eastern China on November 5, 1937. Within weeks the invasion brought several strategic cities on the Chinese mainland under Japanese control, including Beijing and Shanghai.

By 1919, Japanese ambitions had aroused the suspicion of the colonial powers in the region. Britain possessed Malaya, Burma, Singapore, and Hong Kong. The French controlled French Indochina and the Dutch the Dutch East Indies. United States Pacific territories included Hawaii, Guam, and the Philippines.

The United States and Britain felt threatened by Japan's growing power. They were alarmed by Japan's ambitions in China, particularly after the Twenty-One Demands of 1915.

The demands tried to bring China and its vast resources under Japanese control. It also became clear after 1919 that Japan was less interested in acting as a guardian of its new territories, as mandated by the League of Nations, than in exploiting their resources for industrial growth.

Long-standing tensions

There were other causes of tension between Japan and the United States. One related to Japanese immigration. In the late 19th and the early 20th century, thousands of Japanese moved to the United States. They were mainly looking for

The "Twenty-One Demands"

The Japanese government used the distraction of World War I as a cover for trying to take control of China. Unknown to Japan's Western allies, on January 18, 1915, the Japanese sent the Chinese government an ultimatum known as the "Twenty-One Demands." The document was a list of demands that clearly indicated Japanese ambitions to dominate China. Japan wanted effective control over southern Manchuria, Shantung province, and eastern Inner Mongolia. It also asserted that the Chinese had "to engage influential Japanese as political, financial, and military advisers." The demands were backed by the threat of military force. To avoid war, China reluctantly accepted most of the demands, with some modifications. After World War I, however, the Washington Conference of 1921–1922 forced the Japanese to hand back Shantung province.

work in industries on the West Coast. Their arrival prompted a racist reaction from many Americans. They believed that the immigrants were stealing jobs and lowering wages.

An 1894 treaty gave Japanese citizens the right to enter and work in the United States. The U.S. government began to enforce a clause in the treaty forbidding immigration that took jobs away from U.S. citizens.

The Japanese feeling that the Western powers treated them as inferior was reinforced during the Russo–Japanese War. United States president Theodore Roosevelt helped make a peace deal, but the Japanese believed that they did not gain the full rewards for their victory. They blamed the United States. The Japanese felt a similar sense of grievance after the Treaty of Versailles. Again, they believed that their gains were less than those of the other victorious powers.

Aggression and conquest

Japan had defeated the Russian fleet at the Battle of Tsushima in May 1905. It was the first naval defeat by an Asian power of a Western power in the modern period. Japan continued its naval expansion after World War I. The United States and Great Britain were the chief naval powers in the Pacific. Their interests would be threatened by a powerful Japanese Navy. In 1921 and

▶ This Japanese painting shows the Battle of Tsushima in May 1905. Japan's victory over Russia was the first time in the modern period that an Asian power had defeated a European power in a naval battle.

1922, they held a series of conferences in Washington, D.C. The talks aimed to stabilize the naval balance in the Pacific. The Washington Naval Treaty of 1922 placed restrictions on the tonnage of battleships, aircraft carriers, and cruisers that Japan could build in relation to those of the United States and Britain. The ratio was fixed at 5:5:3 for the United States, Britain, and Japan respectively. The United States and Britain argued that they had naval commitments outside of the Pacific, so the Japanese would effectively have equal forces in the Pacific.

Anti-Western feelings

The Japanese came to see the treaty as a source of national humiliation. It was followed by the 1924 Immigration Act. The act stopped all Japanese immigration to the United States, as well as that of other nationalities, particularly from Asia. The Japanese again found the act humiliating.

The Japanese sense of international humiliation had an impact on politics at home. The 1910s and 1920s were a generally liberal period in Japan. Western music and fashions became popular among young, urban Japanese

The Kwantung Army

Also known as the Guandong Army, the Kwantung Army was a regular formation of the Imperial Japanese Army. It was stationed in Kwantung province in Manchuria. It began as a small garrison deployed to the Kwantung Leased Territory, which was a Japanese-controlled region. The garrison defended Japan's commercial interests and protected traffic along the South Manchuria Railroad. In 1919, the garrison was renamed as an army. Its 10,000 troops included an army division, an artillery battalion, and six battalions on railroad guard duties.

In 1931, the Kwantung Army faked a bombing on a train. It then occupied the whole of Manchuria. The Kwantung Army would remain in Manchuria and northern China until the end of World War II, rising to a peak strength of around 700,000 men. However, once the wider conflict broke out, thousands of its soldiers found themselves redeployed to the Pacific theater. The Kwantung Army finally surrendered to the Russians following the Soviet advance into Manchuria in August 1945.

▲ The Kwantung Army grew from a small garrison to become the fearsome formation that occupied Manchuria in 1931.

▲ A convoy of trucks delivers supplies and additional troops for the advancing Kwantung Army in Manchuria in 1931. By February 1932, the region was wholly under Japanese control.

However, many conservatives resented what they saw as Japan's humiliation. Many of them belonged to the military. They thought that the country should turn back to its traditional values. Those values were best summed up by Japan's historic knights, the samurai.

In 1921, a fanatic militarist stabbed to death Japan's moderate prime minister, Takashi Hara. Meanwhile, former soldiers became important members of youth groups, particularly in rural parts of the country. The veterans instilled their militaristic values into young people.

Despite the rise in militarism, politics remained largely liberal. In 1926, Emperor Hirohito came to the throne. He was seen as being pro-Western. Japan also continued to develop a modern economy.

Economic hardship

Japan's prosperity was crippled by a banking collapse in 1927 and the onset of the worldwide Great Depression in 1929. At the same time, the country's population had nearly doubled in size to 56 million in the 50 years before 1920. It had outstripped its supply of natural resources. Most oil, coal, rubber, and metals had to be imported; the United States provided 60 percent of Japan's oil. For Japan's militarists, such dependency was a further blow to national pride. One of the main reasons Japan went to war in 1941 was to try to guarantee its access to natural resources.

Militarists began to argue for aggressive expansion to acquire the raw materials the country needed. They targeted an area that already lay within

Japan's sphere of interest: Manchuria in northern China. The Japanese had acquired trading rights and concessions in the region since 1905. By the late 1920s, Japan controlled the South Manchuria Railroad and exploited Manchuria's natural resources.

The hardliners gain control

The Japanese military increasingly acted outside government control. The army was somewhat more radical than the navy. Army commanders had become used to acting on their own authority at the end of World War I. They had been involved in civil wars in both Russia and China. In 1931, the Imperial Army invaded Manchuria. Its

▲ Priests protest unemployment in Tokyo in the mid-1920s. A huge earthquake in September 1923 worsened the state of the Japanese economy.

Emperor Hirohito (1901–1989)

Although Emperor Hirohito bears some of the blame for the Pacific War, he was in many ways a puppet of the military factions that took over Japan in the 1920s and 1930s. Born on April 29, 1901, he grew into an open-minded and intelligent young man. As a young prince, he traveled to Europe in 1921. He showed more pro-Western tendencies than many of his countrymen. Following his father's death, he became Japan's emperor in 1926. He would hold the position for more than 60 years, making him Japan's longest-reigning monarch.

Hirohito was not an aggressive warmaker. In 1931 he was highly critical of the military takeover of Manchuria. There is also evidence to show that he opposed Japanese alliances with Germany and Italy through the Tripartite Pact. Furthermore, although Hirohito gave his approval for the Pearl Harbor attack in 1941, he does not appear to have been enthusiastic for war with the United States. The fact that the war did occur shows the extent to which Hideki Tojo, the prime minister, was the true center of power in Japan.

On August 15, 1945, after the dropping of atomic bombs on Hiroshima and Nagasaki, Hirohito made a radio address to the Japanese people. He announced Japan's surrender. The Allies did not prosecute Hirohito for war crimes. He lived quietly as emperor until his death in 1989.

▲ Japan's longest-serving monarch, Hirohito reigned from 1926 until 1989.

▲ Students undergo military training in the 1930s. Their machine gun is adapted to fire only blank ammunition.

Railroad on September 18, 1931. The bomb was almost certainly planted by the Japanese, but they blamed Chinese terrorists and invaded. Weakened by civil wars, the Chinese could not resist. By February 1932, the Kwantung Army had taken over Manchuria, which was renamed Manchukuo. For the next five years the Kwantung Army steadily pushed south. It extended its occupation to just north of the Chinese capital, Beijing.

At home, it became increasingly difficult to oppose the army. The militarists won more political power. Extremists assassinated two prime ministers, in 1930 and 1932. In 1933, after international condemnation of the invasion of Manchuria, Japan withdrew from the League of Nations. An attempted military coup in February 1936 failed. The imperial government, however, was dominated by militarists who advocated aggressive territorial expansion.

commanders had no authorization from the government. They calculated that Tokyo would have to approve the invasion once it had happened.

The immediate justification for the invasion was an explosion on the Japanese-controlled South Manchuria

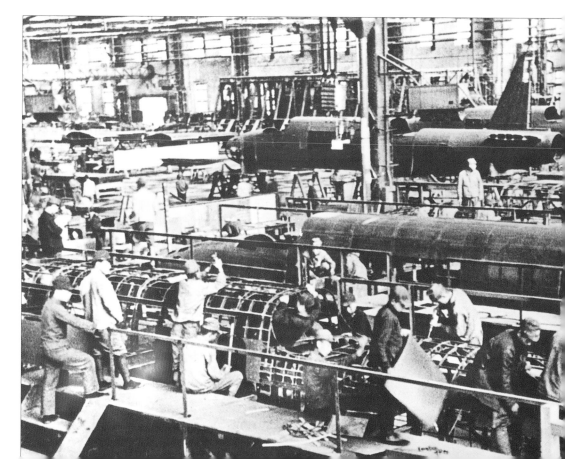

▶ This 1930s photograph shows an aircraft factory in Japanese-controlled Manchuria. Here, Chinese and Japanese workers labored side by side to manufacture Japanese aircraft.

In 1932, Japan had rejected the limitations of the Washington Naval Treaty. In 1937, it began building the world's largest battleships, the *Musashi* and *Yamato*. The military's policies enjoyed wide support among civilians.

By that time the Japanese had also negotiated the Anti-Comintern Pact (1936) with Germany. The pact was later extended to include Italy. The agreement was ostensibly aimed at limiting the spread of communism. It created a defensive alliance against a possible Soviet attack.

China under attack

Japan's militarists launched a massive program of rearmament in the mid–1930s. As a result, the country's need for supplies of natural resources increased.

Military planners sought them in China. In July 1937, Japanese and Chinese troops clashed at the Marco Polo Bridge near Beijing. The episode began the Second Sino Japanese War (there had been a previous war in 1894–1895).

China's Nationalist government was led by Chiang Kai-shek. It was fighting a civil war with communist forces. Much of northern China, meanwhile, was controlled by warlords. The Japanese rapidly occupied most of China's coastal territories and its main cities, including Beijing and Shanghai. Chiang's government fled Nanking shortly before the city fell in December. Japanese troops went on to massacre more than 200,000 civilians in the city.

▲ Chinese, European, and U.S. civilians leave Nanking as the Japanese close in on the city in December 1937. China's Nationalist Army fled the city, leaving its citizens to face Japanese atrocities that became known as the "Rape of Nanking."

11

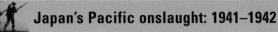
▶ Japanese children celebrate a victory during the Second Sino-Japanese War, which began in 1937. Patriotic displays were common in a country dominated by the military.

The Rape of Nanking

The Rape of Nanking stands out as a notorious war crime even in a century of many atrocities against civilians. It occurred during the Second Sino-Japanese War. The war began on July 7, 1937, with the Japanese invasion of northern China. Nanking was the capital of China's Nationalist government. It had a population of around 700,000 (the numbers were swollen by war refugees). On December 7, as the Japanese closed in, the Nationalists fled. They left Nanking's citizens to their fate.

The Japanese assault on Nanking began on December 10 with huge air and artillery bombardments. By December 15, organized resistance had been crushed. Japanese soldiers began their occupation. In searching for Chinese troops mingling with the civilian population, Japanese troops embarked on nearly two months of unrestrained rape, torture, and murder. Japanese units held murder "competitions" to see who could cut off the most heads. They impaled children on bayonets, and raped around 80,000 women, whom they usually murdered afterward. The killing was supported by the Japanese press.

The slaughter came to an end in February 1938. It was stopped partly to prevent the spread of disease from the many corpses. It also ended as a result of international outrage. Images and descriptions of the killings were smuggled out by Western journalists. In total, up to 200,000 people were killed. The massacre still sours Sino-Japanese relations.

◀ A Chinese family weep in the rubble of their house in Nanking, which was destroyed in a Japanese air raid on the city.

Antagonizing the West

In December 1937, Japanese aircraft sank the gunboat USS *Panay* on the Chang (Yangtze) River in China. The Japanese apologized. They blamed the attack on mistaken identity. The U.S. government, however, acted to curb the Japanese. It sent funds to the Chinese forces, and also increased its own naval power in the Pacific.

In the late 1930s, and again in July 1940, the moderate Prince Konoe was the Japanese prime minister. Real power lay with militarists in his government, however. They included the war minister Hideki Tojo and the foreign minister Yosuke Matsuoka.

After Germany's defeat of France in the war in Europe in June 1940, Japan acquired military rights in Indochina. They set up bases there in return for acknowledging French sovereignty; the French authorities were in no position to resist. The Japanese military presence in Indochina threatened British interests in Burma and Malaya.

Dangerous alliances and grand plans

On September 27, 1940, Matsuoka signed the Tripartite Pact with Germany and Italy. The agreement effectively committed the three to mutual defense in the event of an attack by the Soviet Union or the United States.

The Japanese government also unveiled its plan to create a "Greater East Asia Co-Prosperity Sphere." In theory, the strategy called for East Asia to rid itself of colonial influences and take

▶ Sailors abandon USS *Panay* after the vessel was bombed by Japanese aircraft on the Yangtze River in December 1937. Japanese troops fired on the crewmen as they made their way to shore.

Eyewitness

❝ The mass executions of war prisoners added to the horrors the Japanese brought to Nanking. After killing the Chinese soldiers who threw down their arms and surrendered, the Japanese combed the city for men in civilian garb… suspected of being former soldiers. Just before boarding the ship for Shanghai, the writer watched the execution of 200 men on the Bund [dike]. The killings took 10 minutes. The men were lined against a wall and shot. Then a number of Japanese, armed with pistols, trod nonchalantly around the crumpled bodies, pumping bullets into any that were still kicking. The army men performing the gruesome job had invited navy men from the warships anchored off the Bund to view the scene. A large group of military spectators apparently greatly enjoyed the spectacle.… I witnessed three mass executions of prisoners within a few hours. In one slaughter a tank gun was turned on a group of more than 100 soldiers at a bomb shelter near the Ministry of Communications.… ❞

F. Tillman, reporter for *The New York Times*,
Nanking, December 1937

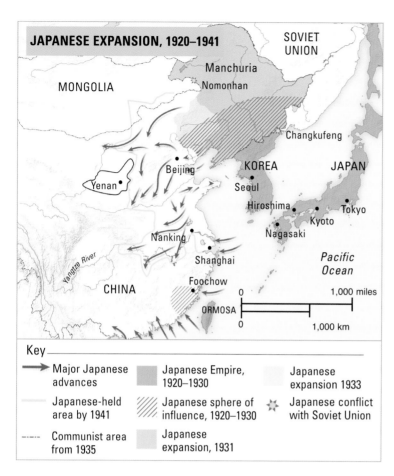

JAPANESE EXPANSION, 1920–1941

SOVIET UNION

MONGOLIA

Manchuria
Nomonhan

Changkufeng

KOREA   JAPAN
Beijing
Yenan
Seoul
Hiroshima   Tokyo
                   Kyoto
Nanking   Nagasaki

Yangtze River
Shanghai   Pacific
CHINA   Foochow   Ocean

FORMOSA
0   1,000 miles
0   1,000 km

Key
→ Major Japanese advances

Japanese-held area by 1941

---- Communist area from 1935

Japanese Empire, 1920–1930

Japanese sphere of influence, 1920–1930

Japanese expansion, 1931

Japanese expansion 1933

✳ Japanese conflict with Soviet Union

▲ Japan's ambition to extend its empire into China met ineffective resistance from divided Chinese forces. It also led to two border clashes with the Soviet Union.

over its own affairs. In reality, it was little more than a Japanese plan to control East Asia and the Pacific—and all of the region's resources.

In reaction to Japan's warlike moves, in July 1940 the U.S. Congress had passed the Two Ocean Naval Expansion Act. The act began a program of warship production. Alarmed Japanese analysts calculated that, by 1944, the U.S. Navy would be more than three times the size of Japan's navy. For Japan to achieve military dominance of the Pacific, it would have to act fast.

In April 1941, Japan signed a non-aggression treaty with the Soviet Union. The treaty freed up much of its army. In July it invaded Indochina. The United States increased its financial aid to China to fight the Japanese. Then, with Britain and the Dutch East Indies, it put an embargo on imports to Japan. The restrictions were potentially catastrophic for Japan. The United States and the Dutch East Indies together provided Japan with some 80 percent of its oil.

Toward war

Japan's military planners saw only two options. They could accept the embargo, but would run out of oil by the end of 1942. Or they could go to war to seize territory in the Pacific and Indian Oceans. That would give them

▶ The *Yamato*, here being fitted out in September 1941, was one of the largest battleships in the world when it was built in 1937.

their own oil supplies. They chose the option that seemed to have the higher chance of success—war.

On October 18, Konoe resigned. He was replaced as prime minister by Hideki Tojo. War planning was already well advanced. Many in the Japanese leadership suspected that Japan could not hope to defeat the United States in a long war. Industrial power would prove decisive in a long conflict. Japan's best chance lay in a rapid victory.

In early November, Tojo proposed a number of diplomatic solutions to the United States. All of his proposals contained suggestions that were almost certain to prove unacceptable, however. They included the resumed sale of aviation fuel to Japan, the U.S. withdrawal from the Philippines, and the stopping of U.S. aid to China. All talks failed. On November 26, the U.S. secretary of state, Cordell Hull, issued his final ultimatums to Tojo. He demanded that the Japanese withdraw from China and Indochina and break their links with the Nazi regime.

The U.S. defiance, however, was now irrelevant. On that same day the Japanese war fleet sailed from positions north of Japan—its destination was Pearl Harbor.

See Also
• World War I and its legacy, Vol.1, p.4
• The United States between the wars, Vol.1, p.26
• The wider world, Vol.1, p.38
• Pearl Harbor, p.16

Prince Konoe (1891–1945)

Prince Fumimaro Konoe was born on October 12, 1891, into a noble family in Tokyo. He began his political career in the 1920s. He was a moderate who initially set himself against the aggressive militarism of the Imperial Japanese Army. On that platform he rose to become prime minister in June 1937. Once in office, however, he found himself unable to resist Japan's growing military expansion. Konoe authorized the 1937 invasion of China, but later tried to negotiate an end to the war. He resigned in January 1939 over his failure to end the conflict and was replaced by Kiichiro Hiranuma.

Konoe retook the prime minister's position on July 17, 1940. He tried using diplomacy to defuse tension between Japan and the United States. When he resigned in October 1941, however, he was replaced by the militaristic Hideki Tojo. Tojo took Japan into the Pacific War in December 1941. Konoe subsequently became an adviser to the imperial court. He committed suicide on December 16, 1945, rather than face war-crimes trials.

▲ The highest-ranking members of the Japanese cabinet—(l–r) Prince Konoe, Foreign Minister Yosuke Matsuoka, Navy Minister Zengo Yoshida, and War Minister Hideki Tojo—discuss policy.

PEARL HARBOR

December 7, 1941, stands in U.S. history as the "day of infamy" when Japan launched a surprise attack on the United States. The attack changed the course of World War II.

The attack on Pearl Harbor had its roots in growing tension between the United States and Japan. Japan had territorial ambitions in the Pacific and in China. It planned to create a "Greater East Asia Co-Prosperity Sphere." The United States had been involved in the Pacific since the late 19th century, when it took control of Hawaii and the Philippines. By 1940, the United States held naval bases across the Pacific.

The chief concern of the U.S. government was that a Japanese advance would threaten Allied, mainly British, possessions in Asia. That would weaken the British cause in World War II and aid Germany. Germany and Japan had signed a pact agreeing to come to each other's defense in the event of attack.

Roosevelt's strategy

The government of Franklin D. Roosevelt courted China as an ally. It thought the Chinese could help deter

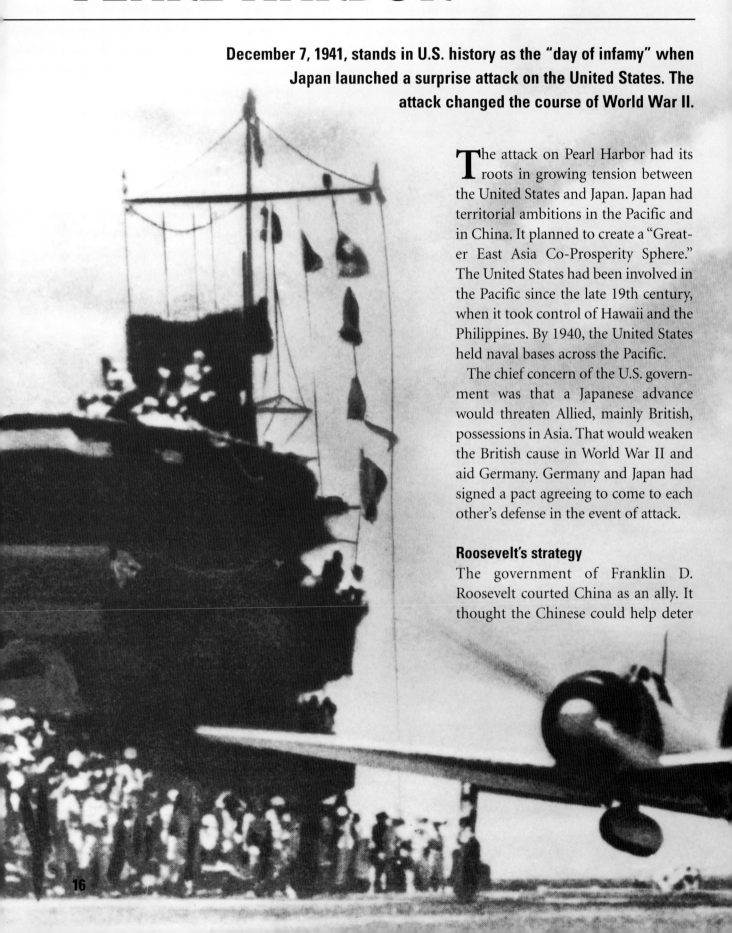

Japanese aggression. The United States provided the Nationalist government in China with trade credits and supplies. In May 1940, Roosevelt also sent the Pacific Fleet to Pearl Harbor on Hawaii in the Central Pacific. He aimed to deter Japanese aggression against British and Dutch possessions in Southeast Asia. Pearl Harbor became the largest U.S. outpost in the Pacific.

Diplomatic negotiations

As tension grew between the United States and Japan, diplomatic movements continued. In February 1941, Japan sent a new ambassador to the United States, Kichisaburo Nomura. Nomura wanted peace, but later historians have questioned whether his government shared his commitment. In March, Nomura began talks with U.S. secretary of state Cordell Hull about China, which Japan had invaded in 1937. Hull demanded a Japanese withdrawal from China, and the talks made little progress. Meanwhile, the Japanese continued their military build-up. Many Japanese politicians believed war was inevitable.

Imposing trade restrictions

In July 1941, Japan agreed with Vichy France that it could station 50,000 troops in French Indochina. (Vichy France was the part of France not occupied by Germany.) This put the Japanese army and navy within striking distance of Malaya, the Dutch East Indies, and the Philippines. They belonged to Britain, the Netherlands, and the United States respectively.

Roosevelt responded by freezing all Japanese assets in the United States. On August 1, he placed an embargo on oil exports to Japan, which depended on imported oil. Roosevelt also ordered General Douglas MacArthur to return to active duty, creating a new U.S. Army Forces Far East in the Philippines. Faced with this tough U.S. stance, the Japanese tried to initiate high-level talks. The United States insisted that Japan stop its expansionist activities, and the talks broke down. Ultimately the oil embargo was one of the major factors that drove Japan to attack the United States in 1941.

Formulating a plan

When the embargo came into effect, the Japanese military had enough oil for only 18 months of combat. Prime minister Hideki Tojo considered options for a rapid campaign. He eventually decided on simultaneous attacks on the Philippines and Malaya, followed by an invasion of the Dutch East Indies to capture oil reserves.

The U.S. Navy remained a sticking point, however. Japan's war plans envisioned allowing the U.S. fleet to sail into the Central Pacific. There, the Imperial Japanese Navy would ambush and destroy it. Combined Fleet commander Admiral Isoroku Yamamoto thought the plan was bound to fail.

▼ Japanese sailors line the decks of an aircraft carrier as Mitsubishi A6M Reisen ("Zero") fighters take off for Pearl Harbor on December 7, 1941.

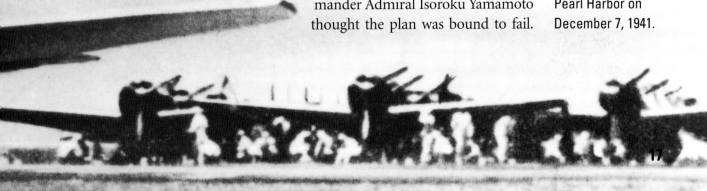

In early 1941 he proposed the "Pearl Harbor Plan," for a surprise attack on Hawaii. Yamamoto had been educated at Harvard and knew the potential industrial strength of the United States. He thought that Japan would be unwise to instigate a war. If it did, however, he saw the Pearl Harbor plan as the only way forward.

Buying time

Yamamoto planned a strike on the U.S. base at Pearl Harbor on Oahu Island. It would cripple the U.S. Navy, and delay any possible U.S. attack on the Japanese home islands by at least a year. The Japanese could then use the time to capture other U.S. bases and set up a defensive perimeter in the Pacific. The perimeter would allow them to exploit oil and rubber supplies in the "Southern Resource Area," centered on the Dutch East Indies. Tojo ordered the attack on December 4, 1941.

The operation begins

On December 6, Roosevelt made a final appeal for peace to the emperor. By now, however, the plan to attack Pearl Harbor was underway. Six aircraft carriers and two battleships had sailed from the Japanese Kurile Islands on November 26. They were commanded by Admiral Chuichi Nagumo. Maintaining radio silence to avoid detection, the task force sailed across the Pacific. It reached a position 230 miles (370km) north of Pearl Harbor. Everything was ready.

Historians still debate how much the Allies knew about the coming attack. Some argue that the Allies likely intercepted Japanese signals but failed to put them together into an overall picture. On November 30, U.S. intelligence decrypted a message from Tokyo to Berlin. It warned of imminent war: "There is extreme danger that war may suddenly break out between the Anglo-Saxon nations and Japan [and] this war may come quicker than anyone dreams." The message did not, however, contain any reason for U.S. military leaders to suspect that Hawaii was the target.

A final warning

Early on December 7, in Washington, D.C., U.S. Naval Intelligence intercepted a message from Japan telling

Isoroku Yamamoto (1884–1943)

Admiral Isoroku Yamamoto was one of Japan's leading naval strategists. Considering the possibility of war with the United States, he remarked, "If in the face of such odds we decide to go to war—or rather are forced to do so by the trend of events—I can see little hope of success in any ordinary strategy." Yamamoto had traveled extensively in the United States, both as a student and later as a naval attaché. Understanding the industrial power of the United States, he went to war in 1941 with great trepidation.

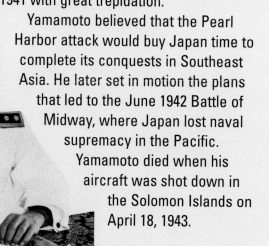

Yamamoto believed that the Pearl Harbor attack would buy Japan time to complete its conquests in Southeast Asia. He later set in motion the plans that led to the June 1942 Battle of Midway, where Japan lost naval supremacy in the Pacific. Yamamoto died when his aircraft was shot down in the Solomon Islands on April 18, 1943.

◄ Admiral Yamamoto had misgivings about entering into war with the United States.

Ambassador Nomura to break off negotiations with Cordell Hull. Army Intelligence decoded another message, sent at the same time. It ordered Nomura to submit his message to the State Department at precisely 1:00 P.M. (7:00 A.M. Hawaii time) and to destroy his code machines.

Army Intelligence concluded that a U.S. base in East Asia would soon be attacked. It tried to reach Army chief of staff General George C. Marshall. Marshall was not reached until two hours later; he issued a warning to all U.S. forces to be on the alert. The message to Hawaii was delayed, however. The War Department had to send it by commercial telegraph because radio communications with the island were out of service. The message only reached the U.S. Army commander in Hawaii, Walter C. Short, after the attack.

An easy target

Without a warning, the U.S. forces on Oahu were not ready to face an attack. They had not organized an effective defense. Several reports had identified an air raid as the most likely form of attack, probably in the early morning. Short and the U.S. Navy commander in Hawaii, Admiral Husband E. Kimmel, however, were more worried about the threat of sabotage. They had grouped ships together to make them easier to guard. For the same reason, the island's 400 aircraft were parked wing to wing on the airfields. However, this would make them an easy target for Japanese pilots. Both Short

▲ Japanese fighter pilots ready their planes on the aircraft carrier *Akagi*, 230 miles (370km) north of Pearl Harbor. They headed to Hickam Field to attack U.S. airplanes on the ground and stop them from getting into the air.

◄ Admiral Chuichi Nagumo, a key figure in tactical development in the Imperial Japanese Navy, commanded the Carrier Strike Force during the attack on Pearl Harbor.

▲ This aerial photograph of Pearl Harbor, taken during the attack of December 7, 1941, shows the inviting target the assembled U.S. warships offered Japanese pilots.

and Kimmel would lose their commands after the attack—unfairly, in the opinion of many historians.

Inside the anchorage at Pearl Harbor were 96 ships. They included the pride of the Pacific Fleet along Battleship Row: *Arizona*, *California*, *Iowa*, *Maryland*, *Nevada*, *Oklahoma*, *Tennessee*, *Utah*, *West Virginia*, and *Iowa*. The aircraft carriers *Lexington* and *Enterprise* were at sea, delivering aircraft to bases on Wake and Midway islands.

Incoming aircraft detected

The first part of the Japanese strike force took off from the carriers before dawn. It included 181 fighters, dive-bombers, and torpedo bombers. It was divided into four groups to head for the key targets: the anchorage at Pearl

Harbor itself, and the airfields at Kaneohe, Hickam, and Wheeler Field.

At 7:02 A.M., a radar station in the north of Oahu detected 137 inbound aircraft and reported them to the Army Operations Center. The duty officer, Kermit Tyler, was a fighter pilot with no radar experience. He and a switchboard operator were the only people on duty. Tyler believed the aircraft to be B-17 bombers due from the mainland. He told the radar operator, "Don't worry about it." The radar station then shut down for the day as scheduled.

Tora! Tora! Tora!

As the Japanese aircraft approached Oahu, the USS *Ward*, a destroyer on routine patrol, attacked a midget submarine at the entrance to Pearl Harbor.

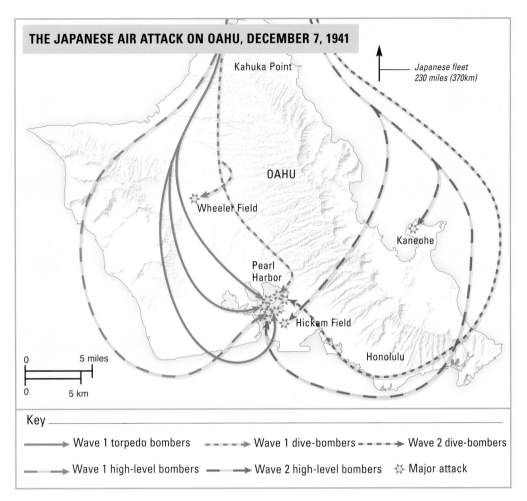

THE JAPANESE AIR ATTACK ON OAHU, DECEMBER 7, 1941

Kahuka Point

Japanese fleet
230 miles (370km)

OAHU

Wheeler Field

Kaneohe

Pearl
Harbor

Hickam Field

Honolulu

0   5 miles

0   5 km

Key

→ Wave 1 torpedo bombers   ---→ Wave 1 dive-bombers   ---→ Wave 2 dive-bombers

→ Wave 1 high-level bombers   ─→ Wave 2 high-level bombers   ✲ Major attack

◀ The paths taken by the two arms of the Japanese attack targeted the island's airfields as well as the harbor itself.

The craft was one of five intended to torpedo ships once the air attack had started. News of the incident reached Kimmel and his Pacific Fleet staff. They requested confirmation of the report.

Commander Mitsuo Fuchida led the strike force above Oahu. At 7:53 A.M., he radioed back to the fleet the code words "*Tora! Tora! Tora!*" ("Tiger! Tiger! Tiger!"). The message meant that the Japanese had achieved complete surprise. Fuchida could not believe what he saw. He later recalled: "I have seen our own warships assembled for review before the emperor, but I have never seen ships, even in the deepest peace, anchored at a distance less than 500 to 1,000 yards from each other…. This picture down there was hard to comprehend."

The attack began as soldiers, sailors, and Marines went about their Sunday-morning routines. Dive-bombers and

Eyewitness

❝ It was just like the newsreels of Europe, only worse. We saw a bunch of soldiers come running full tilt toward us from the barracks and just then a whole line of bombs fell behind them knocking them all to the ground…. A bunch of soldiers had come into our garage to hide. They were entirely taken by surprise and most of them didn't even have a gun or anything. One of them asked for a drink of water…. He had just been so close to where a bomb fell that he had been showered with debris. ❞

Ginger, U.S. schoolgirl,
Hawaii, 1941

fighters hit the air bases. The torpedo bombers headed for the fleet. They carried weapons specially redesigned for the shallow anchorage.

On Battleship Row, the *Arizona*, *California*, and *Oklahoma* suffered several direct hits, caught fire, and sank. More than 1,100 of the *Arizona*'s 1,500 crew were killed. Many were trapped below decks and drowned. The *West Virginia*, meanwhile, was holed and took on a huge amount of water. It tipped severely to one side. The ship's captain ordered the flooding of the other side of the ship, to bring it back upright. The maneuver allowed many of the crew to escape before the vessel eventually sank.

The air bases suffered similar destruction. Squadrons of flying boats at the Kaneohe Bay naval air base were destroyed on the ground. The same happened to fighters at Hickam, Wheeler, and Bellows fields.

The flight of B-17 Flying Fortresses due from the mainland arrived at the height of the attack. They had been stripped of weapons and ammunition for the long flight to Hawaii and had no defenses. However, the B-17s survived to land successfully at Hickam Field.

Mass destruction

The reaction of the U.S. forces to the attack was heroic but ineffective. The commander of the battleship *Nevada* got the ship under way as the attack began. It took only 45 minutes instead of the usual two hours. *Nevada* fired its antiaircraft guns as it steamed down the channel. On the *West Virginia*, African American cook Doris "Dorie"

▼ Smoke billows from the USS *West Virginia* after the Japanese attack. The ship sank, but was later salvaged. The *Tennessee*, beyond the *West Virginia*, was less seriously damaged; its crew fought to control fires on nearby ships.

◀ Rescuers stand on the upturned hull of the USS *Oklahoma* in the aftermath of the Japanese attack. A total of 429 sailors died when the battleship capsized. The USS *Maryland*, in the background, was also damaged, but not severely.

Miller manned an antiaircraft gun, for which he had no training. He won the Navy Cross for his brave action.

The attacked ended at 8:30 A.M. The island's defenders took the chance to improve their readiness. When a second wave of 170 planes arrived at 9:00 A.M., antiaircraft crews downed 20 of them. Many more got through, however, damaging ships in dry dock.

A devastating raid

When the attackers departed at 10:00 A.M., they left a scene of destruction. Five battleships were sunk or sinking. Eight more ships were damaged. Some 320 airplanes had been destroyed or damaged, and the runways of the air bases were cratered and littered with wreckage. Black smoke hung over the harbor and the airfields. There were 2,335 men killed and more than 1,000 wounded. Burning oil slicks covered the harbor. They hampered recovery crews who raced to

rescue men trapped underwater. Japanese losses, meanwhile, were between 30 and 60 aircraft, the five midget submarines, and fewer than 100 men.

"A date which will live in infamy"

It was early afternoon on the U.S. East Coast when word of the attack began to come in. Nomura had been unable

▼ Sailors abandon the USS *California* as it begins to sink. In the background, largely obscured by smoke, is the upturned hull of the capsized *Oklahoma*.

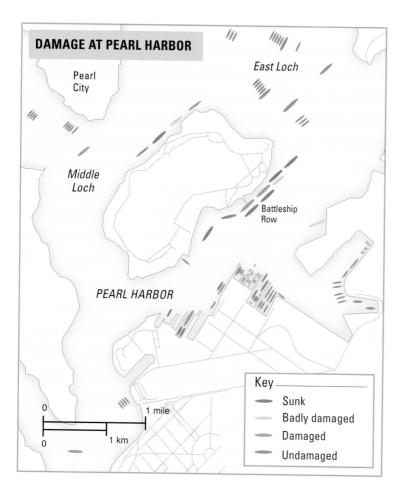

DAMAGE AT PEARL HARBOR

Pearl City

East Loch

Middle Loch

Battleship Row

PEARL HARBOR

0   1 mile

0   1 km

Key

- Sunk
- Badly damaged
- Damaged
- Undamaged

to deliver his message at 1:00 P.M., as his government had instructed. He arrived at the State Department only after the attack had begun. Roosevelt met with his military advisers. In the next 24 hours, they received reports of attacks on other U.S. and Allied bases in the Pacific: Guam, Wake Island, Hong Kong, and Singapore.

Roosevelt drafted a request for a declaration of war against Japan. He delivered the request in a six-minute address to Congress at noon on December 8: "Yesterday, December 7, 1941, a date which will live in infamy, the United States of America was suddenly and deliberately attacked by naval and air forces of the Empire of Japan." The Senate voted unanimously to declare war; in the House of Representatives, only Senator Jeannette Rankin of Montana voted against going to war.

▲ This diagram shows where U.S. vessels were sunk or damaged. Most of the five battleships lost were sunk in the first wave of the attack.

▶ A guard of honor fires a salute over a mass grave for victims of the Pearl Harbor attack at the air base at Kaneohe.

The reaction to Pearl Harbor in the rest of the country was initially one of panic. On the West Coast, in particular, many people expected an imminent Japanese attack. In San Francisco, the National Guard began patrolling the Golden Gate Bridge. People filled the streets. They fired guns at passing aircraft and smashed car headlights and street lamps to create a blackout. The Federal Bureau of Investigation (FBI) arrested Japanese American men and held them in prison for several days. There were also a series of unprovoked civilian attacks on individual Japanese Americans, or Nisei. Such attacks would be followed within months by the organized large-scale internment of Japanese Americans.

A change of tactics

The damage to Pearl Harbor and its facilities was severe, but the attack had not affected the Pacific Fleet as badly as the Japanese had hoped. The bombs hit none of the massive refueling facilities at Pearl Harbor. Neither did they seriously damage its dry docks and repair yards. The fleet would be

Wake Island

Wake Island was a small U.S. Navy outpost in the Western Pacific. The island was a coral atoll with a 5,000-foot (1.5km) airstrip. It was defended by 450 men led by Major J.P.S. Devereux, and a Marine fighter squadron.

Japanese bombers struck Wake on December 8, 1941. They destroyed most of the fighter planes, although the Japanese also lost many aircraft to coastal guns. When the Japanese tried to land on December 11, U.S. gun crews damaged or sank several ships. The Japanese troop convoy turned back. News of the successful defense elated the U.S. public.

The Japanese continued with daily bombings, however, while the arrival of a U.S. relief force was delayed. When the Japanese landing force returned on December 23, the defenders, outnumbered five to one, surrendered.

Control of Wake Island was strategically vital to the Japanese. It allowed them to set up a secure line of communication across the Central Pacific. This isolated the Philippines and exposed Douglas MacArthur's forces there to attack.

▲ On Wake Island, U.S. aircraft lie destroyed after the Japanese raid of 1941. Although U.S. troops fought off the first attacks, they were eventually forced to surrender.

operations. In effect, the attack forced the U.S. Navy to modernize its tactics. It could not depend on the big guns of battleships. The dominant weapon in naval combat for the rest of the war would be carrier-borne aircraft. The "flattops" and their pilots would stop the Japanese advance in the Coral Sea and win decisive victories at Midway, the Philippine Sea, and Leyte Gulf later in the war.

The United States joins the war

The most important legacies of the Pearl Harbor attack were strategic and emotional. Anger over the attack finally ensured that Americans abandoned their isolationism. They backed the country's entry into the war, two years after fighting had broken out in Europe. Jeannette Rankin's vote against war—she had taken a similar stand before the United States entered World War I—this time cost her her political career. "Remember Pearl Harbor!" became a rallying cry,

▲ Jeannette Rankin was the only Senator to vote against war. Her pacifism was out of step with the views of the public after the attack on Pearl Harbor.

able to use the yards throughout the war to repair damaged ships. More significantly, perhaps, the U.S. aircraft carriers had escaped the attack. That meant that the Pacific Fleet still had the ability to carry out long-range

▶ On December 8, 1941, President Roosevelt asks Congress for a declaration of war against Japan. The president's "Infamy" speech was broadcast around the world. Within half an hour, the United States was at war.

spurring industrial production and military efforts.

On December 11, meanwhile, Adolf Hitler declared war on the United States. Although Germany and Japan were members of the Tripartite Pact, there was no real reason Hitler had to declare war at this stage. His reasons for doing so remain uncertain. He probably believed that war with the United States was inevitable at some time. He was said to be elated when news came through of Pearl Harbor, because he saw the Japanese as strong allies.

Benefits to the Allies

Hitler's decision meant that Roosevelt was able to enter the war in Europe without encountering any domestic opposition. The benefit to the rest of the Allies of the full entry of the United States into the war was obvious. The "arsenal of democracy" brought the Allies new supplies of resources, industrial strength, vast reserves of personnel, and stronger political

What did Roosevelt know?

The greatest controversy surrounding Pearl Harbor concerns how much Franklin D. Roosevelt knew of Japanese plans before the attack. Several historians have suggested that Roosevelt ignored warnings about the attack from U.S. intelligence. They say he wanted an excuse to take the United States into the war.

One main controversy concerns the difference between Roosevelt having a sense that an attack might be imminent, which he may have had, and his having specific knowledge that Pearl Harbor was the target and not warning the military there, which is very unlikely. There were many rumors in Washington, D.C., that war was coming. The most likely explanation is that the president and his advisers did expect an attack, but that they believed it would be against British and Dutch colonies in East and Southeast Asia, rather than against the U.S. Pacific Fleet.

leadership. In a well-known—but probably inaccurate—story, British prime minister Winston Churchill, was woken up to learn the news of the attack at Pearl Harbor. He remarked, "Well, we've won then!" In a few hours, the attack had begun the process of turning the United States into the leader of the Allied coalition.

See Also
- The approach of war, p.4
- The defeat of the British and Dutch, p.28

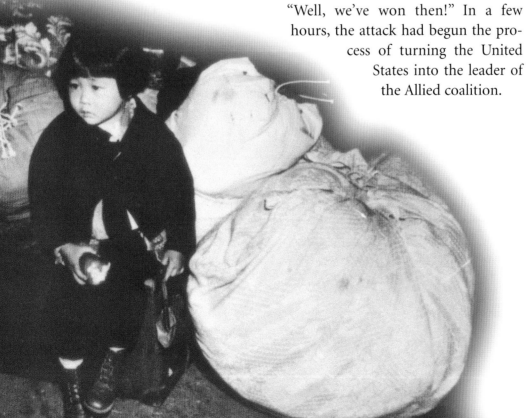

◀ The Pearl Harbor attack provoked a backlash against Japanese Americans, such as this girl waiting to be sent to an internment camp in 1942.

THE DEFEAT OF THE BRITISH AND DUTCH

The attack on Pearl Harbor was just the start of Japan's campaign of conquest in the Pacific. Its commanders launched a rapid onslaught against Allied forces to secure a series of conquests in the region.

▶ British troops erect barbed-wire defenses along Hong Kong's rocky shore.

Many Japanese officers understood that there were great risks in a long war against the United States and Britain. Admiral Isoroku Yamamoto was commander of the Combined Fleet. He thought that the Japanese might have the advantage for six months in the Pacific. Then the industrial power of the United States would come to bear on the conflict.

The Japanese developed a short-term strategy to achieve their long-term goals. They aimed to aquire territories that were rich in resources or strategically important. Their targets included the Dutch East Indies (now Indonesia) and the British colonies of Malaya, Singapore, Hong Kong, and Burma, as well as the U.S.-ruled Philippines. They also aimed to create a line of defenses to protect the captured territory and the Japanese home islands.

The defensive perimeter was to stretch from the Kurile Islands south to Rabaul on New Britain. It would pass through Wake Island, the Marianas, the Carolinas, the Marshalls, and the Gilberts. From Rabaul, it would extend west to northwestern New Guinea, taking in the East Indies, Malaya, Thailand, and Burma.

The Japanese thought that the Allies would wear themselves out attacking this perimeter. They would eventually negotiate peace, and leave Japan in possession of its conquests. The plan depended on speed. For six months after the attack on Pearl Harbor on December 7, 1941, the Japanese forces swept all before them.

The first defeats

On December 8 (the same day as the Pearl Harbor attack, but on the other side of the international date line), Japan invaded Thailand and northern Malaya. It also attacked Hong Kong. Japanese infantry occupied some smaller islands in the Philippines. Aircraft launched attacks on the U.S. garrison on Wake Island, midway between the Philippines and Hawaii. By December 13, the Japanese had driven British defenders from the New Territories on the Chinese mainland to the island of Hong Kong. Overnight on December 18/19, the Japanese landed on the island. After hard fighting, the British surrendered on Christmas Day.

Strenuous defense

On Wake Island, meanwhile, the 450 U.S. Marines had put up a strong defense. When the Japanese sent a

The sinking of the *Prince of Wales* and *Repulse*

In October 1941, Britain sent a force of warships to protect the waters around Malaya and Singapore in the event of a war with Japan. British prime minister Winston Churchill sent the brand-new battleship HMS *Prince of Wales*, the battle cruiser HMS *Repulse*, and four destroyers. The force was named "Force Z." It was commanded by Vice Admiral Sir Tom Phillips. It arrived at Singapore on December 2. Only six days later, the Japanese invaded Malaya.

Phillips sailed his ships up the Malaya coast. He aimed to stop the Japanese from making amphibious landings to the north. It was a high-risk strategy: Force Z would have no air cover against Japanese attack aircraft and would be outnumbered by Japanese vessels.

On December 9, Force Z was spotted by Japanese aircraft. Phillips decided that the risks were too great and turned his fleet back. It was too late, however. A Japanese force of 52 torpedo planes and 34 bombers soon attacked. Torpedoes struck both the *Prince of Wales* and the *Repulse*; within hours, both had sunk. The losses were a huge blow to the pride of the British Royal Navy, for decades the world's most powerful navy. Churchill later said, "In all the war, I never received a more direct shock."

▲ British seamen scramble over the side of the torpedoed HMS *Prince of Wales* before the ship finally sinks on December 9, 1941.

landing fleet to the island on December 11, U.S. aircraft and artillery sank two destroyers and a transport ship. They forced the fleet to withdraw. Under heavy bombardment, the Wake Island garrison held out until December 23, when the Japanese put troops ashore.

By Christmas, Japanese forces had taken control of other Pacific territory, such as the Gilbert Islands. On the Asian mainland, meanwhile, they were about to inflict on the British one of the worst defeats in their military history.

Fighting the British

The Japanese attack began on the night of December 7/8 with two amphibious landings. One division landed in Thailand, just north of the border with Malaya. Another landed on Malaya's northeastern coast. The Japanese forces had about 60,000 men in total. They advanced in two columns. One headed down the east of the country, the down the west.

Facing the advance was a force of British and Commonwealth troops led

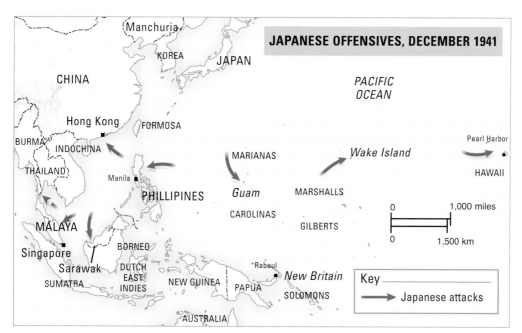

JAPANESE OFFENSIVES, DECEMBER 1941

◄ Japan launched a series of attacks across Southeast Asia in 1941 to seize strategic bases and economic resources.

by Lieutenant-General Arthur Percival. With 88,000 men, Percival had more troops than the Japanese, but the Japanese were better armed. They also had 459 modern aircraft and 80 tanks. The British had no armor and only 158 aircraft, many of which were old.

The Japanese troops were trained in jungle warfare, and included many combat veterans. By contrast the Allied soldiers had no special training. Be-lieving the jungle to be impenetrable, for example, the British set up road blocks to stop the Japanese. The Japanese simply moved off the roads and advanced through the vegetation.

Thailand and Malaya

North of the Malayan border, Japan secured control of Thailand, which surrendered on December 9. In Malaya, meanwhile, Japanese troops made

◄ Japanese soldiers advance along a jungle road with their supplies loaded onto bicycles. The use of bicycles greatly increased the mobility and speed of the Japanese advance in Southeast Asia.

Yamashita, the Tiger of Malaya (1885–1946)____

General Tomoyuki Yamashita became known as "the Tiger of Malaya" after his eight-week victory over Allied forces there. He began his military career in 1906 as an infantry officer. His intelligence and resolve saw him rise through the ranks of the military and political establishment in Japan. Yamashita led units in Korea and Manchuria before being appointed commander of the Twenty-Fifth Army in November 1941. After his victory in Malaya in January 1942, he was promoted to full general. Prime Minister Hideki Tojo—a long-standing political rival—then posted him to Manchuria, far from the main conflict. After Tojo resigned in July 1944, Yamashita commanded the defense of the Philippines.

He surrendered on September 2, 1945.

After the war, Yamashita was found guilty of war crimes committed by his troops in Manila, the Philippine capital. He was hanged on February 23, 1946. It is now widely accepted that he knew nothing about the atrocities.

▲ Tomoyuki Yamashita became a national hero in Japan after his victory over Allied troops in Malaya.

swift progress down the mainland. They gained control of oil fields in the north of the country. The Japanese were highly mobile. They covered ground quickly, even in thick jungle. They made a series of amphibious "jumps" along the coast to get behind the British front line. The destruction of a powerful Royal Navy force by the Japanese on December 9 meant that the British could not oppose these landings.

The Japanese took the town of Jitra on December 12. They swept south to break a line of Allied defenses along the Slim River. The British retreated south toward the capital, Kuala Lumpur, where Percival had his headquarters. Between January 1 and 10, 1942, more Japanese amphibious landings outflanked the Allied defensive line near the town of Kampar. Kampar fell on January 3, and the Japanese came to within 20 miles (32km) of Kuala Lumpur. The British abandoned the capital, which fell on January 11.

Japan had conquered two-thirds of Malaya, a remarkable achievement. The rapid advance had resulted in the decimation of British air units. Around 100 British aircraft were lost in the first week. It had also brought the Japanese control of captured airfields. They extended their superior air cover south toward the end of the Malay peninsula and Singapore.

Local Allied resistance briefly helped to raise morale among the retreating Allies. It did little to slow the pace of the Japanese advance, however. The Allies were driven back toward Johor, the southern tip of Malaya.

Retreat to Singapore

Defeat in mainland Malaya was now a virtual certainty. Allied forces had only one place to retreat to: Singapore, just off the southern tip of the peninsula. Although only 266 square miles (683 sq km), the island was one of Britain's most important colonies in East Asia. It had become a British territory in 1824, and had grown into a thriving commercial and military port. The island gave Britain command of vital sea routes to the Dutch East Indies, India, and Australia.

Singapore's importance was reflected in the batteries of naval guns that protected it. However, the guns were

◀ Japanese troops advance through a rubber plantation in Malaya in 1942. Malaya was a major producer of rubber, a material crucial to Japan's industrial needs.

▼ A British infantryman surrenders during the Japanese advance in Malaya.

useless to repel the Japanese. They were set up to face a seaward attack. The Japanese assault came from mainland Malaya. More crucially, the guns and their ammunition were designed for firing at ships over long distances, not for antipersonnel use.

The British defense of Malaya ended on January 31, 1942. The last British troops crossed the Johor Strait to Singapore. The defeat had cost the British 4,000 dead and 21,000 prisoners, against Japanese losses of 2,000 dead and 3,000 wounded.

Defending Singapore

Percival allocated his men to defensive positions on Singapore. It seemed as if the British might now have the advantage. Percival had received reinforcements. At the beginning of February, his total troop numbers were around

▶ Japanese troops celebrate their rapid conquest of Malaya with a captured railroad locomotive.

▼ Japanese troops come ashore from a landing craft during the Malaya campaign. Their skill at amphibious landings was a key factor in their rapid progress.

85,000. The Japanese commander Tomoyuki Yamashita had only 35,000 troops, although he had greater air and armor resources. Yet British commanders were concerned about defending Singapore. Percival was warned about its defensive weaknesses by his superior General Sir Archibald Wavell, the Allied Supreme Commander in East Asia. Wavell was concerned about the northwest of the island. Understrength Australian battalions were guarding a long stretch of coastline there. Percival made a fatal error in his defensive plans, however. He concentrated his forces in order to defend naval and air installations on the east of the island. When the Japanese attacked, they came from the west.

Assault on Singapore

The Japanese assault on Singapore began on the night of February 8–9. Infantry of the Japanese 5th and 18th Divisions crossed the Johor Strait. They attacked the Australians in the northwest, as Wavell had feared. There was vicious fighting, often at close quarters. The Australians fought back the first two Japanese landing forces. However, a third force secured a beachhead and began to push the Allies inland.

The next night, troops of the Japanese Imperial Guards Division crossed the strait and attacked in the northwest. The first attacks were stopped on the beaches. A confused order from a local commander then led the Allied defenders to withdraw. They fell back to the Jurong Line, a defensive line across the center of the island. The mistake allowed Japanese troops to get ashore without resistance. They began to overwhelm the island.

The fall of Singapore

In Singapore City itself, civilians panicked under constant bombing and shelling. The Jurong Line was the last hope for an effective defense, but the Japanese broke through on February 11. They captured the island's main water reservoirs the next day. This gave them a crucial advantage. If they cut off water supplies, dehydration might cause many deaths.

On February 15, Percival met his senior officers. Unknown to them, Yamashita's forces had been weakened by the weeks of fighting. They possibly would not have had the strength to overwhelm the island's defenders had they put up a prolonged fight. After pessimistic reports at the

commanders' conference, however, Percival decided to surrender.

About 130,000 British, Commonwealth, and Malay soldiers were taken prisoner. They represented a large proportion of British military strength in Asia.

Eyewitness

❝ Dodging bombs and shells, I eventually approached the city [Singapore]. Hundreds of unburied dead almost blocked the streets, and the smell of putrefying flesh mingling with the bombed sewerage was appalling. A huge black pall of smoke from the blazing oil tanks on Pulau Bukum and the Naval Base hung over the city, and the rain drops were turning black as they reached the ground. Fires blazed everywhere, wrecked cars littered the streets with the dead, Jap planes bombed at will, and armed soldiers were wandering about bewildered; what unbelievable chaos. ❞

R.G. Curry, lieutenant commander, British Royal Navy
Singapore City, February 12, 1942

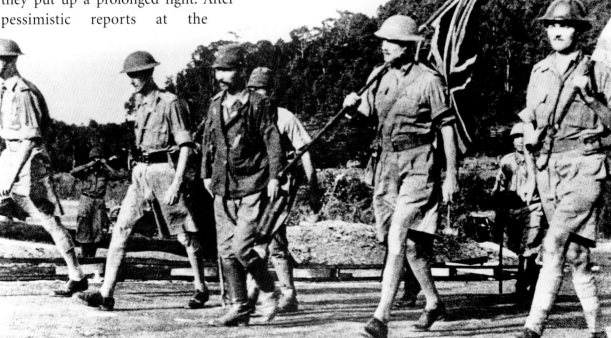

▼ The British surrender at Singapore on February 15, 1942.

Bushido: the way of the warrior _____

Bushido means "the way of the warrior." It was an ancient Japanese code of behavior. It was developed from the 11th to the 14th centuries by the class of knights called samurai. Bushido's values were complex, and many were not written down. They involved complete obedience to leaders, a total contempt for death and pain, and a mastery of military skills. The values of Bushido were revived during the 1920s and 1930s. The military leaders who became increasingly influential in Japan turned to them as the basis for a return to a former age of national pride.

The values of Bushido underlay Japanese military training and produced determined troops. Recruits were put through brutal training; they were also taught that death was preferable to surrender. That principle cost both the Japanese and the Allies heavy casualties during the Pacific War. It also underlay Japan's adoption of suicide tactics (kamikaze) toward the end of the conflict. General William Slim, British commander in Burma, wrote: "If 500 Japanese were ordered to hold a position, we had to kill 495 before it was ours—and the last five killed themselves. It was this combination of obedience and ferocity that made the Japanese army, whatever its condition, so formidable."

Another by-product of Bushido was cruelty toward Allied prisoners and conquered civilian populations.

◀ Students in samurai armor parade at a *seinengakko*—a school where Japanese boys learned to fight, usually in preparation for military service.

Yamashita had suffered around 5,000 casualties. The victory was a spectacular achievement for the Japanese and an unmitigated disaster for the Allies.

Strengthening Allied territories

The British were not the only Allies to suffer defeats by the Japanese. South and east of Malaya lay the islands of the Dutch East Indies. They stretched across 2,000 miles (3,200km) of the Pacific Ocean. One of Japan's major war aims was to get control of the islands' oil and other resources. It also wanted the colony's ports as bases for naval actions in the South Pacific and the Indian Ocean.

The islands were protected by around 140,000 soldiers of different nationalities. The majority of the troops were local people who had little training and no experience of battle. Only 25,000 troops were Dutch. The troops were controlled by ABDACOM (American-British-Dutch-Australian Command), under the overall command of British general Archibald Wavell. ABDACOM was intended to coordinate Allied military and other resources in East Asia. In the case of the Dutch East Indies, though, these resources were relatively low. The most powerful force in the area was a flotilla of six cruisers commanded by Dutch rear admiral Karel Doorman.

The attack on the Dutch East Indies

The Japanese had made significant landings in mid-December 1941 in Sarawak on Borneo, one of the largest islands of the Dutch East Indies. Their main offensive began in January 1942. It involved three Japanese forces. Western Force would attack Sumatra, Java, and British North Borneo. Eastern Force would strike at the islands of Celebes and Amboina before advancing into the far south of the Dutch East Indies. Central Force aimed to take Borneo.

The offensive began on January 10, 1942. Initial operations went smoothly, despite some localized resistance. By the end of January, Japan had conquered the coastlines of almost all of the central and eastern islands. A landing at Balikpapan on January 24 brought most of Borneo's oil fields under Japanese control.

Futile resistance

In February the Japanese widened their operations. On February 14, Western Force began its attacks on Sumatra. It made extensive parachute landings around Palembang. British and Commonwealth defenders met the paratroopers with heavy anti-aircraft fire. The next day, the Allies launched an air attack against a Japanese amphibious landing. It sank one ship, killing dozens of men. The Allies wasted their successes, however, by making a premature withdrawal.

Java and the Java Sea

By the end of February, much of central and southern Sumatra was in Japanese hands. On March 1, Japanese forces made major landings along the northern coast of Java.

The decisive moment of the conquest of the Dutch East Indies was one of the largest naval battles since World War I: the battle of the Java Sea. On February 27, Doorman sent five cruisers and nine destroyers to intercept a Japanese invasion force off Java. Protecting the Japanese force were 4 cruisers and 14 destroyers.

The battle began in the late afternoon. Although the forces were relatively evenly matched, the Japanese were skilled at fighting at night. They also had stocks of fast long-range torpedos. The British cruiser HMS *Exeter* was hit by a Japanese shell, but remained afloat. Soon after, the Dutch destroyer *Kortenar* was hit by a torpedo. It blew up before sinking. The destroyer HMS *Electra* was hit by shells and sank.

By about 6:30 P.M., Doorman's force was greatly reduced. Four U.S. destroyers had to leave the combat area to refuel. Nevertheless, the rear admiral took his remaining vessels to hunt out the Japanese force in the darkness. It was a disastrous decision. HMS *Jupiter* struck a mine and blew

▼ On occupying a new area in the Dutch East Indies, Japanese soldiers set up a post office.

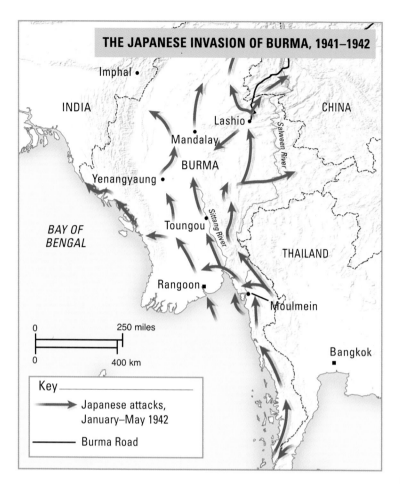

THE JAPANESE INVASION OF BURMA, 1941–1942

Imphal •
INDIA
Lashio •
Mandalay •
BURMA
Yenangyaung •
Salween River
Toungou •
Sittang River
BAY OF
BENGAL
THAILAND
Rangoon ■
Moulmein •
Bangkok ■
CHINA

0   250 miles
0   400 km

Key
→ Japanese attacks,
January–May 1942
— Burma Road

Plans in Burma

In mainland Southeast Asia, the Japanese had invaded Burma in December 1941. They wanted to control the British colony to protect the Japanese invasion of Malaya. They would be able to stop British troops advancing from British India to the west. Burma would also provide a potential starting place for an invasion of India itself.

Burma was defended by about 27,000 troops, but many of them were of poor quality. The far north of the country was protected by the Chinese. Two Chinese divisions were led by the U.S. commander "Vinegar" Joe Stilwell. Allied air support was virtually nonexistent. Nevertheless, the Allies expected the Japanese to make slow progress. Burma had mountainous jungles divided by rivers that would provide good defensive positions.

▲ The rapid Japanese advances through Burma drove the British back into India and the Chinese back into China.

up. When the Allies found the Japanese vessels, torpedo attacks sank the *De Ruyter* and the *Java*. Doorman died in the attack on *De Ruyter*. Five more Allied ships were sunk in the next two days. The disaster marked the virtual end of resistance to Japan's conquest of the Dutch East Indies. All the islands had surrendered by March 8.

The Burma campaign

In December 1941, Japanese forces invaded the far south of Burma from Thailand. They were followed on January 20, 1942, by the main invasion force. This was the Japanese Fifteenth Army. It comprised about 35,000 men led by General Shojira Iida. The Japanese overran the town of Kawkareik. They pushed north toward the

▶ The Dutch flagship *De Ruyter* was sunk in the Battle of the Java Sea. The action was disastrous for the Allied defense of the Dutch East Indies.

◄ Indian troops in the British Army advance through a plantation during the campaign in Malaya.

Burmese capital, Rangoon, which lay in the southern half of the country. By January 26, the Japanese had reached Moulmein. British resistance in the town collapsed on January 30.

Major-General John Smyth commanded the 17th Indian Division. He argued that all Allied troops should pull back to the Sittang River. The river would form a natural defense to break up the assault. The British high command hesitated. They did not agree to the plan until February 19. By then the Japanese had inflicted heavy losses on the British defenders around the Salween and Bilin rivers.

Fighting in the jungle

The jungles of Southeast Asia presented unique challenges for fighting. The dense foliage made travel difficult. The heat and humidity caused heat exhaustion and increased the need for constant supplies of water. Once off the few, unreliable roads, most supplies were carried by soldiers and mules. In the monsoon season, landslides and flash floods made the jungle even more treacherous.

Jungle fighting was confusing. Normal tactical maneuvers were impossible and it was difficult to keep visual contact with other units. Ambushes were a constant danger, and the dense foliage could deflect bullets and shells. But the most serious problem was disease. At one point in the Burma campaign, the British had 14 men sick for every one injured in battle; 90 percent of the sick suffered from malaria. Fungus and bacteria thrived. Even the smallest cut could become infected.

◄ Japanese soldiers in the Malay jungle support a makeshift bridge to enable their comrades to cross a river.

Japanese amphibious forces

A key element in Japan's rapid victories in 1941 and 1942 was amphibious warfare. Japan's commanders had developed equipment and tactics for landing forces from the sea, as they did, for example, during the invasion of China in 1937. One specialty was night landings, for which troops and vehicles were marked with luminous paint. The Japanese also had specialized equipment. Collapsible boats carried up to nine men, while larger landing barges carried up to 120 men or a small tank or artillery piece. For bridging rivers, troops each carried a pontoon float; when a number were put together, they formed an improvised bridge.

During the course of the war, the United States developed its own amphibious forces. Soon they outclassed the Japanese, with bigger landing craft and amphibious vehicles, and superior technology and tactics.

◀ Japanese amphibious troops run ashore on beaches in Borneo in January 1942.

The Allied retreat from Burma

When the Allied fallback did begin, both sides raced to reach the main bridge across the Sittang in the town of the same name. After hand-to-hand fighting around the river, the Allies managed to blow up the bridge before the Japanese could cross. The action also left thousands of Allies stranded on the wrong side of the river, however. The 17th Indian Division lost 5,000 men killed or captured.

Lieutenant-General Thomas Hutton, in charge of Burma, ordered that Rangoon be abandoned. Wavell disagreed. He replaced Hutton with Lieutenant-General Sir Harold Alexander. Alexander agreed with Hutton, however. "Burcorps," as the British and Allied forces were known, continued their retreat. Rangoon fell to the Japanese on March 8.

Reinforcements arrived from the Chinese Fifth and Sixth Armies, but they were defeated at Toungou on March 30. On May 1, the Japanese took Mandalay. The city was nearly 1,000 miles (1,600km) north of where the campaign had begun. Alexander realized that defending Burma was impossible. On April 25, he ordered Burcorps to retreat to India. The remaining Chinese forces would head back to their homeland.

The Alied retreat to India

The retreat to India was one of the longest in British military history:

Why did everyone underestimate the Japanese? _____

The Japanese conquests of 1941 and 1942 stunned the Allies. U.S. and British leaders had badly underestimated their foe, mainly on the basis of racial stereotypes. In the 1930s, Japanese forces were seen as fanatical warriors who could not match the discipline and courage of Western troops. One popular myth was that the short average height of the Japanese and the shape of their eyes made them poor fighters who could not aim weapons properly. Even after Pearl Harbor, an assumption remained that Allied troops would easily dominate in land fighting.

As a consequence, Allied defenses and training were neglected. The Allies also failed to appreciate Japanese advances in military technology and training. They particularly misjudged Japan's carrier airpower. The Allies paid a high price for their racist thinking. It was only when they started to respect their enemy that they began to work out how to defeat them.

See Also
• Pearl Harbor, p.16
• The fall of the Philippines, p.42
• Life under Japanese occupation, p.54

▼ U.S. tanks are unloaded at the docks of Rangoon at the start of the ill-fated Allied defense of Burma.

over 600 miles (1,000km) in nine weeks. The first Allied units entered India on May 19. They were weakened by aerial attack, ground combat, and disease. Burcorps had lost a total of 13,000 men in Burma, compared to 5,000 Japanese casualties.

In only six months the Japanese had won a stunning series of victories in Southeast Asia. The Dutch and British colonial empires had collapsed. In air, sea, and land warfare the Imperial Japanese forces had proved manifestly superior to their enemies.

◄ Smoke billows from burning oil refineries near the docks at Rangoon after the Allies retreated from the Burmese capital in March 1942.

THE FALL OF THE PHILIPPINES

The capture of the Philippines was a crucial part of Japan's strategy to secure an empire in the Southwest Pacific and to remove U.S. power from the region. Hours after Pearl Harbor, Japan attacked the islands.

The Philippines are a group of some 7,000 islands in the Pacific. They were of great strategic importance because they lay between Japan on one hand and Southeast Asia and the islands of the Dutch East Indies (Indonesia) on the other. Those territories were rich in resources that the Japanese needed, such as oil. With the region under its control, Japan could then move southeast to secure bases on New Guinea and the Solomon Islands. Japanese possession of the Solomons would limit communications between Australia and the United States. That would hamper Allied operations in the Southwest Pacific.

A U.S. colony

The Philippines became a U.S. colony in 1898, at the end of the Spanish–American War. The U.S. Navy began to use Manila Bay. Located off Luzon,

the largest and most northerly of the Philippine islands, the bay was one of the finest fleet anchorages in Asia.

By the mid-1930s, however, the U.S. Navy was short of funds. There were few ships at the naval base. The United States had also stopped building fortifications in the Philippines under the 1922 Washington Naval Treaty. The treaty was intended to reduce tensions in the Pacific. As a result, only the islands near the entrance to Manila Bay were well protected.

In any case, the U.S. government planned to withdraw from the Philippines. It could not defend a colony 3,000 miles (5,000km) from the nearest U.S. base on Hawaii. It gave the Filipinos some self-government in 1935, and promised full independence in 1946. In the meantime, defense of the islands would be handed over gradually to the Philippine government, despite its limited resources.

Growing Japanese power

Meanwhile Japanese power grew, isolating the Philippines. To the north Japan had colonized Formosa (Taiwan). To the east, it had taken over the Palau, Caroline, and Marshall islands as part of the Versailles Treaty of 1919. Japan's possessions east of the Philippines formed a chain broken only by two U.S.-controlled islands: Guam and Wake. In 1939 Japan struck west, across the South China Sea. Japanese troops occupied the island of Hainan in January. In July 1941 they entered southern French Indochina (modern Vietnam). By mid-1941, the Philippines were threatened on three sides.

▼ Japanese troops land on the island of Corregidor on May 6, 1942. Corregidor, the last U.S. stronghold in the Philippines, fell to the Japanese later in the day.

U.S response

As diplomatic relations with Japan deteriorated, military and political leaders in Washington, D.C., decided to reinforce the Philippines. They rushed to create defenses to counter a Japanese attack that was starting to seem inevitable.

In July 1941, U.S. leaders appointed General Douglas MacArthur to head a new command in the region. It was named U.S. Army Forces in the Far East (USAFFE). MacArthur was a famed but controversial commander who had retired from the U.S. Army. He was in the Philippines acting as a military adviser to the president, Manuel Quezon. To defend some 115,000 square miles (300,000 sq km) of territory, MacArthur had only 12,000 men of the Philippine Division, 4,000

men of the Philippine Army, and 20,000 Filipino "irregulars," trained militia. The number of recruits were significantly higher by December.

The Philippine Division was led by General Jonathan Wainwright. It comprised the U.S. Army-trained

▲ Filipino Scouts load a 10-inch gun on a U.S ship. The U.S.-trained Scouts were key to defending the Philippines.

Douglas MacArthur (1880–1964)

After graduating at the top of his class from the U.S. Military Academy at West Point in 1903, Douglas MacArthur served his first posting in the Philippines. His career advanced rapidly. By 1913, he was a member of the U.S. Army's general staff. After World War I, he became superintendent of West Point. He was again posted to the Philippines, but returned to Washington in 1930 to serve as the chief of staff. Although he retired in 1937, MacArthur was recalled in July 1941 to command the U.S. Army Forces in the Far East. Having said that he could defend the Philippines, MacArthur took

▲ General MacArthur was appointed head of forces in the Southwest Pacific in 1942.

Japan's invasion as a blow to his integrity. On Corregidor he made it clear that he was willing to fight on. However, the Allies needed a supreme commander in Southeast Asia to organize the fight against the Japanese. Roosevelt ordered MacArthur to leave the Philippines. He left for Australia on March 12, 1942. After a week-long journey, he arrived to tell reporters: "I have come through and I shall return." His men fought on for another two months. "I shall return" became a catchphrase for MacArthur, and a public declaration of his zeal to liberate the Philippines, which colored his view of strategic aims throughout the war.

Philippine Scouts, led by U.S. officers, together with the only U.S. Army unit in the Philippines, the 31st Infantry Regiment, which numbered some 2,100 men.

War Plan Orange

MacArthur inherited a defense plan for the Philippines known as War Plan Orange. It had last been updated in April 1941. The plan recommended defending only Manila Bay. The U.S. garrison in Manila, the capital, would withdraw to the Bataan Peninsula and the fortified island of Corregidor. The plan reflected Japan's strength and the weakness of the islands' defenses. U.S. military commanders had decided that most of the Philippines must be sacrificed if the Japanese attacked.

MacArthur, however, wanted to cancel War Plan Orange. He urged his superiors to adopt an ambitious program to build up the Philippines as a stronghold of U.S. power. MacArthur called for some 200,000 men. Because he had only limited naval resources available, he also called for the creation of a huge air force in the islands. MacArthur wanted hundreds of the new Boeing B-17 bomber, which was later known as the "Flying Fortress." The bombers would to be able to attack Japanese bases on Formosa and any approaching invasion fleet.

U.S. chief of staff George C. Marshall gave top priority to reinforcing and equipping USAFFE. MacArthur hoped that the program could be in place by 1942. He did not take into account the logistical problems of building up and supporting large forces so far from the United States, however. A shortage of cargo space on military ships delayed shipments across the Pacific.

The U.S. Far East Air Force

MacArthur's plan to gain air superiority had influential support. Senior officers in the United States Army Air Force (USAAF) were eager to prove the value of high-altitude bombing. By the late summer of 1941, all new U.S. warplanes not earmarked for Britain and Russia in their fight against Germany were scheduled to go to the Philippines. By the middle of 1942, MacArthur would have four bomber groups of 314 aircraft and two fighter groups of 260 aircraft. The new force, the U.S. Far East Air Force, would be led by General Lewis H. Brereton. He arrived on Luzon in late 1941.

As warplanes arrived on Luzon, however, so warships left. The U.S. Navy's small Asiatic Fleet was

▼ U.S. defense of the Philippines was concentrated around Manila Bay on the northern island of Luzon.

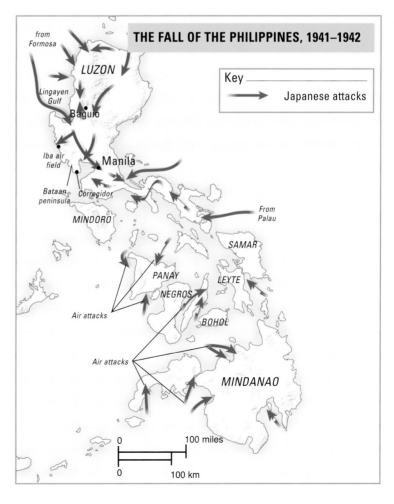

The myth of invincibility

Before the fall of Singapore, many British and U.S. planners believed that Japanese soldiers would be too physically weak to beat Western troops. In fact, the troops of the Imperial Japanese Army were battle-hardened veterans. They had learned a strict code of warfare. Their officers had studied at jungle-warfare school. They learned concealment and how to infiltrate enemy flanks. In December 1941, when the Japanese attacked in Southeast Asia, the Allies were unable to withstand their offensives. Another myth soon developed that the Japanese were jungle-fighting supermen. The view began to change only in late 1942. By then, the Allies had won victories in New Guinea and on Guadalcanal. Allied troops now underwent jungle training and new units were created, such as U.S. Marine Raider battalions.

dispersed from Luzon south to Mindanao and to Borneo, in the Dutch East Indies, to avoid air attack. The naval presence on Luzon was reduced to a dozen patrol boats, although there were still 29 submarines, 32 patrol aircraft, and the 4th Marine Regiment.

A force to be reckoned with

By December 1941, MacArthur's army had grown in size to more than 19,000 U.S. soldiers and 12,000 Philippine Scouts. A further 100,000 Filipino militia were under training. MacArthur organized his troops in four groups: Northern Luzon Forces, under Wainwright; Southern Luzon Forces, under General George Parker; a Reserve Force to protect Manila; and a force to defend the southern Philippines.

MacArthur's air force now had about 270 aircraft. They included 100 modern Curtiss P-40 Warhawk fighters and 35 B-17s. He was expecting 128 more bombers by February. A convoy was

▲ Japanese soldiers were disciplined, skilled, and prepared to fight to the death.

▶ Douglas MacArthur (right) and General Jonathan Wainwright discuss the defense of Luzon.

also due to bring another 70 fighters, an artillery brigade, hundreds of vehicles, and thousands of tons of supplies.

The potential of the growing air force was limited, however. The islands lacked airfields and maintenance facilities. They also had poor antiaircraft defenses. That left aircraft on the ground vulnerable to attack. Despite such problems, MacArthur estimated that he would be able to meet any invasion by summer 1942.

The Japanese prepare to strike

MacArthur did not have that long. By November 1941, the Japanese had moved an invasion force of General Masaharu Homma's Fourteenth Army from China to Formosa. On December 4, a heavily defended convoy left Formosa carrying 43,000 men. Meanwhile the Japanese had assembled a powerful force of 500 aircraft on Formosa. They planned a surprise attack on Luzon to destroy Brereton's air force on the ground and clear the way for a landing.

The first Japanese air raids were scheduled for dawn on December 8. Given the time difference, that would be only three or four hours after the attack on Pearl Harbor, some 3,000 miles (4,800 km) away. However, heavy fog over Formosa prevented the aircraft from taking off.

▼ Japanese troops pass through a burned out Filipino town, one of many settlements wiped out in the fighting to conquer the islands.

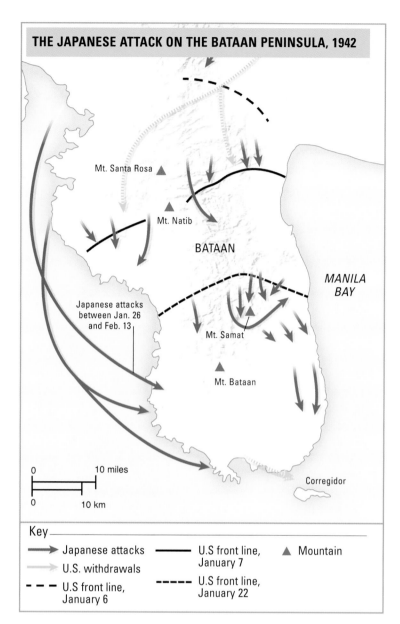

THE JAPANESE ATTACK ON THE BATAAN PENINSULA, 1942

Mt. Santa Rosa ▲

Mt. Natib ▲

BATAAN

MANILA
BAY

Japanese attacks
between Jan. 26
and Feb. 13

Mt. Samat ▲

▲ Mt. Bataan

0   10 miles

0   10 km

Corregidor

Key

→ Japanese attacks — U.S front line,
January 7   ▲ Mountain

→ U.S. withdrawals

- - - U.S. front line,
January 6   ----- U.S. front line,
January 22

▲ The Bataan
Peninsula was
mountainous and
covered with dense
jungle. The only
escape route was to
the tiny fortified
island of Corregidor.

Devastating aerial attack

By 3:30 A.M., news of the attack on
Pearl Harbor had reached MacArthur.
He ordered his troops to battle
stations. It was only much later in the
morning that he sent a reconnaissance
flight to Formosa, however. By the
time he authorized a bombing raid on
the Japanese bases at lunchtime, it was
too late. The fog over Formosa had
cleared hours earlier. Some 200 Japanese warplanes were now approaching
the B-17 base at Clark Field, 75 miles
(120km) north of Manila.

The Japanese caught 18 U.S. B-17s on
the gound and a number of P-40
fighters just taking off. Within an hour,
they had destroyed all the B-17s and
more than half of the P-40s. Elsewhere
the Japanese launched air raids against
Iba Field in northwest Luzon; Baguio,
the so-called summer capital of the
Philippines; and Mindanao. By the end
of the day, the U.S. Far East Air Force
had lost half of its aircraft.

Japanese raids began again next day.
Within 24 hours they had destroyed
seven more airfields and a naval base.
Brereton withdrew his remaining B-
17s to Mindanao to organize attacks
on Japanese convoys off Luzon's
northern coast.

Japanese troop landings

That same day, Japanese troops landed
on the north and northwest coasts of
Luzon. They were small forces sent to
capture airfields, but their effect on
the militia was devastating: The
Filipinos fell back in confusion. Their
retreat ended MacArthur's hope of
defeating the Japanese on the beaches.

The main Japanese landing took
place on December 22. Homma's 48th
Division came ashore at Lingayen
Gulf, 120 miles (195km) northwest of
Manila. Striking inland, it cut off the
northern part of Luzon and began to
advance on Manila and Bataan.

Withdrawal to Bataan

MacArthur ordered his troops to
withdraw into Bataan. On December
23, a second Japanese division landed
at Lamon Bay, south of Manila. It
advanced north. MacArthur's forces
were now cut off on two sides.

Communications began to collapse
as U.S. and Filipino units streamed

back toward the Bataan Peninsula. The command structure was kept in place by Wainwright and the commander of the Southern Luzon Force, George Parker. Parker fought a staged withdrawal. Homma held off some of his forces, because he thought he would have to fight for Manila. Instead, on December 26, MacArthur declared Manila an open city. He moved his headquarters onto the island of Corregidor and told his commanders that Plan Orange was now in effect.

Trapped on Bataan

The Japanese entered Manila on January 2, 1942. On January, 5 U.S. and Filippino forces completed their withdrawal into Bataan. About 80,000 troops and more than 25,000 civilians were trapped on a mountainous peninsula covered in jungle. Bataan was 14 miles (22km) wide and 30 miles (45km) long. It had no escape route.

▲ A landing craft full of Japanese soldiers approaches the burning city of Manila late in December 1941.

◄ Wearing British-syle helmets that were replaced later in the war, U.S. troops survey the damage caused by a Japanese air raid on the Philippine town of Paranaque in December 1941.

Corregidor

The island of Corregidor lies about 25 miles (40km) west of Manila and 2 miles (3.2km) east of the tip of the Bataan Peninsula. It covers an area of 3.5 square miles (9sqkm) and partly blocks the western entrance to Manila Bay. The United States began to fortify Corregidor as early as 1905. It was part of a chain of defenses to protect the bay and its anchorage from naval attack.

The U.S. Army transformed the rocky island into a stronghold they dubbed Fort Mills. By 1941, the defenses consisted of 14 gun batteries concentrated on the western side of the island. To the east rose Malinta Hill. An underground headquarters and hospital complex was built into the hill in 1938. Known as the Malinta Tunnel, it was 1,400 feet (425m) long and 30 feet (9m) wide. It had 25 secondary tunnels. East of the tunnel, the land rose to a small airfield known as Kindley Field. Elsewhere on the surface there were barracks, a parade ground, a power plant, and two docks. There was even a golf course and an electric railroad. The peacetime garrison was about 6,000 men.

▲ Bombs explode on Fort Drum, a fortified island defending Corregidor, in spring 1942.

In their rapid withdrawal, U.S. and Filipino troops had left behind most of their equipment. They had very limited supplies in Bataan. As a result of MacArthur's plan to defend all of the Philippines, food, ammunition, weapons, and medical supplies were widely dispersed. United States and Filipino troops in Bataan were on half-rations; within weeks they were eating mules.

United States and Filipino forces set up defenses across the neck of the peninsula. The west was defended by I Corps under Wainwright, and the east was held by II Corps under Parker. Between them lay Mount Natib, over 4,000 feet (1,220m) high. A second line was set up 8 miles (13km) south, in front of two more high points.

The campaign for Bataan

Japanese forces were weakened after their advance. Homma had suffered nearly 7,000 casualties, and a malaria epidemic had left 13,000 men sick. A division also had been transferred to the Dutch East Indies. He was reinforced by only one inexperienced brigade. Still, Homma launched his first attack on Bataan on January 9. He had promised that he could conquer the Philippines in 45 days. He would lose face if his campaign stalled.

MacArthur remained confident that his troops could hold out. On January 10, he left Corregidor to inspect the Bataan defenses. It was his only visit to the peninsula: His preference for staying on Corregidor led his troops to nickname him "Dugout Doug."

Bataan Death March

The Japanese took more than 12,000 American and 60,000 Filipino prisoners on Bataan. They were to be held at a camp more than 100 miles (160km) north. The Allies had been on starvation rations for months. They were exhausted and sick from malaria and dysentery. The Japanese forced them to march all day, without food or water, in 95°F (35°C) heat. Prisoners who fell behind were executed. What became known as the Bataan Death March began on April 10 and lasted a week.

The survivors were packed into airless railcars for an eight-hour journey. They were then marched another 8 miles (13km) to the camp. Of the 72,000 prisoners, some 18,000 died. General Homma, the Japanese commander who ordered the march, was arrested after the war. He was tried, found guilty of murder, and executed in April 1946.

Japanese progress

The first line of U.S. defenses held until January 15, when the Japanese found a route over Mount Natib. They attacked the flank of Parker's II Corps. They then infiltrated Wainwright's position from behind. The U.S. forces withdrew to the second defensive line on January 22. At the same time, Homma attempted three amphibious landings on the west coast of the peninsula behind the U.S. and Filipino positions. All three landings were thrown back with heavy losses.

▲ American troops await their fate after surrendering to the Japanese in Bataan on April 9, 1942.

▼ American prisoners leaving Bataan carry sick comrades in improvised stretchers.

▶ A Japanese assault team uses a flame thrower against a U.S. position during the attack on Corregidor.

The second defensive line held, but by the end of February the Bataan defenders were on starvation rations. Most were suffering from malnutrition, malaria, or dysentery. The U.S. government told MacArthur that his troops could not be rescued. Neither could they surrender, however. The government wanted to show a sign of U.S. determination to fight. At the same time, it did not want to risk having such an important commander as MacArthur captured by the enemy. He was evacuated to Australia on March 12, making a famous promise to the Filipinos: "I shall return." Wainwright took command of U.S. forces in the Philippines.

Meanwhile Homma received two new divisions of troops. His strengthened forces launched a fresh attack on April 3. Exhausted, the defenders finally broke. Wainwright withdrew to Corregidor to organize what few defenses remained in the Philippines. He left General Edward King to hold out as long as he could in Bataan. On April 9, despite a radio call from MacArthur ordering Wainwright to launch a counterattack, King accepted the hopelessness of the situation and surrendered his forces.

Eyewitness

❝ By the time we got to about the third day [of the Bataan Death March], we knew that they [the Japanese] were just hoping all of us would die. Hell, they hadn't even given us a drink of water. By then the people really started to fall out. A guy would jump into a ditch for a little bit of water. They'd run a bayonet through you, or shoot you, or hit you in the head with a shovel, whatever way they could to dispose of you. Behind us they had a cordon of tanks. If you stopped, those tanks would ground you into the dirt. The Japs also had this group we called the Buzzard Squad. They killed those that couldn't keep up. ❞

John Emerick, U.S. serviceman,
Bataan, Philippines

Corregidor stands alone

Corregidor now stood alone in the Philippines. Survivors from Bataan had increased its garrison to more than 11,000. Water, food, and medical supplies were running out. Homma could have waited and starved the defenders into submission. His pride drove him to take the island by force, however. Corregidor had been under air attack since the end of March. Homma now ordered an artillery bombardment from Bataan. On May 1, a huge artillery barrage wrecked what few defensive positions were left on the surface. Only underground defenses remained. During the night of May 3–4, a U.S. submarine arrived to remove the last evacuees.

Wainwright stayed on Corregidor. Early on May 6, Japanese troops and three tanks landed on the eastern end of the island. The fighting moved west,

around the entrance to the Malinta Tunnel, the U.S. headquarters. The defenders held the Japanese back until midday. Wainwright was concerned for the 1,000 wounded in the Malinta Tunnel. He surrendered.

Homma forced Wainwright to order all U.S. and Filipino forces in the islands to surrender. He threatened to kill the Corregidor garrison if he did not. On May 8 Wainwright broadcast the order across the Philippines. It was a humiliating end to a brave defense.

▲ Japanese soldiers celebrate their conquest of the Philippine islands in April 1942.

◀ General Jonathan Wainwright broadcasts news of the U.S. surrender on May 8, 1942. He later received the Medal of Honor for his part in the defense of Bataan and Corregidor.

See Also
• Life under Japanese occupation, p.54
• The Battle of Leyte Gulf, Vol.9, p.16
• Retaking the Philippines, 1944–1945: Vol.9, p.36

LIFE UNDER JAPANESE OCCUPATION

The Japanese conquest of Southeast Asia changed the lives of people in the area beyond recognition. Prisoners of war, civilians, women, and children were often treated very badly.

The Japanese presented their take-over in Southeast Asia as an anti-Western and anticolonial crusade. They told local populations that they would be free from exploitation. The region would enjoy freedom and wealth within the Greater East Asia Co-Prosperity Sphere led by Japan.

Breaking the Geneva Convention

The Japanese used their hundreds of thousands of prisoners of war (POWs) as part of their propaganda campaign. In the Philippines and Singapore, they put Allied POWs on public parade. They wanted to show the Asian population Western weakness and the superiority of the Japanese military. Such acts breached the terms of the Geneva Convention, the internationally accepted rules of conduct during wartime. Under the convention, POWs should be treated with respect for their person and honor.

The convention also states that POWs must be paid for any work they do. The work they are made to do must not be dangerous, unhealthy, or degrading. The Japanese did not follow the rules. They used thousands of Allied soldiers as slave labor in steel mills, coal mines, shipyards, and factories. The brutal treatment reflected the Japanese attitude that soldiers who surrendered did not deserve respect. It also reinforced the inferiority of former colonial masters and the control that the Japanese empire had over them.

▲ These prisoners of war in a Japanese camp are painfully thin. Their physical state is the result of harsh treatment and short rations during captivity.

Japan's plan for Southeast Asia

The Japanese planned to unite the conquered nations of Southeast Asia into a new self-sustaining economic community. It would be named the Greater East Asia Co-Prosperity Sphere. The plan made Japan's military takeover sound like the founding of a new trade organization. In reality, however, the Co-Prosperity Sphere was no more than a cover. It hid the looting of the region's natural resources. Months before the war began, in July 1941, politicians in Tokyo realized that Japan had to secure Southeast Asia's resources if it was to win a war against the United States. Japan especially needed oil, rubber, and tin. The politicians called the region Japan's "first sphere of supply."

The Co-Prosperity Sphere was part of an elaborate propaganda exercise. It aimed to convince the peoples of Southeast Asia that Japan's military aggression was part of a great anticolonial movement. It would create a new "Asia for the Asians." The reality was very different. The Southeast Asian states lost their economic independence, and trade collapsed. By 1945, food production across the region had all but failed. Millions of people were poor and starving.

Encouraging nationalism

It was a major Japanese goal to destroy Western influence across Southeast Asia. For that reason, they imprisoned all Allied civilians as well as military personnel. However, replacing the various colonial governments in the region proved more difficult.

Before the start of the war, the Japanese had begun to encourage nationalist groups that wanted self-rule. In Thailand in 1941, they started training a group of Burmese nationalists to support an eventual invasion of Burma. The group would form the core of the Burmese Independence Army (BIA). The BIA only had 2,300 members. The Japanese meant it to show the Burmese that they had come not to invade, but to bring independence from the British. The illusion was reinforced in June 1942. The Japanese installed a puppet regime under the Burmese nationalist Ba Maw. By then the Japanese army effectively controlled the country.

The BIA changes sides

The BIA's commander, Aung San, realized that the Japanese regarded the Burmese as racially inferior. Under Japanese occupation, the economy also suffered. Rice exports fell to less than half the prewar levels and economic growth ground to a halt. Most Burmese lived in abject poverty.

At the end of 1942, Aung San began secret talks with the British. Three years later, the British and Indians advanced south into central Burma in May 1945. Aung San marched his troops out of Rangoon to meet them. On his order, his men turned against the Japanese. They dispersed into the countryside to fight as a pro-Allied partisan army.

Filipino opposition

The Philippines were in a different political position from other colonies. Their governing power—the United

▶ General Aung San, commander of the Burmese Independence Army. Aung San held secret talks with the British government to drive the Japanese out of Burma.

States—had given the islands some self-government in the 1930s. The United States had also promised independence by 1946. The Filipinos rejected the type of independence offered by the Japanese. They saw that it was a form of military occupation.

The Japanese entered Manila, the Philippine capital, in January 1942. President Manuel Quezon had gone into exile after Pearl Harbor. He left behind José Laurel, a Supreme Court justice who had studied in Tokyo. Quezon told Laurel to offer his services to the Japanese, but to look out for the best interests of the Filipinos. Laurel drafted a new constitution. It decreed that only those sympathetic to Japan could serve in the government. The constitution banned all democratic political activity. The Philippines became a Japanese puppet state. The three years of military rule were

▶ Filipinos pose near a list of Japanese rules for civilian behavior in the islands.

marked by curfews, blackouts, and indoctrination. The period also saw a growth in guerrilla activities by Filipinos. They became more effective at sabotaging their Japanese governors.

Political maneuvering in the DEI

The Japanese had more success in the Dutch East Indies. They planned to eradicate the Dutch presence by appealing to the local population's desire for self-rule. The Japanese asked the nationalists Mohammad Hatta

▲ Burmese people gather by the roadside to watch Japanese troops march toward the capital, Rangoon, in June 1942.

and Sukarno to form a government. They imprisoned the Dutch civilian population. They also shut down Dutch newspapers and magazines, and banned the Dutch language.

The new government had no power. It answered to the Japanese army, which set out to exploit local resources for the Japanese war effort. Food and other necessities grew scarce. Locals suffered misery and starvation. The Japanese also forced up to four million Indonesians (known as *romusha*) to labor on construction projects both at home and in other territories. Several thousand *romusha* died as a result of the appalling working conditions.

▲ After the war, Sukarno led the Indonesian nationalist campaign for independence from the Netherlands.

Subhas Chandra Bose and the Indian National Army

In April 1941, Indian nationalist Subhas Chandra Bose (1897–1945) traveled to Berlin to meet Adolf Hitler. Bose hoped to make an alliance to overthrow British rule in India.

The Japanese knew that Indian nationalists could be used against the British. During the invasion of Malaya, they recruited Indian prisoners of war to form the Indian National Army (INA). Some Indians joined from a sincere belief in independence; others joined simply to avoid forced labor. However, in December 1942, plans for the INA stalled.

Bose gave the INA a new lease on life. He realized that he was achieving nothing in Germany. In May 1943, he traveled back to Asia. With the support of Japanese prime

▲ Bose believed that India's independence from Britain could be won through armed force, which would come from siding with Germany and Japan.

minister Hideki Tojo, he took control of the INA. Bose won political and financial support from Indians across Japan's conquered territories. He obtained new recruits—not just prisoners of war, but also young men from expatriate families.

In November 1943, the 40,000-strong INA moved north to Burma and began combat operations. In early 1944 it joined the Japanese offensive into northeast India. Bose saw the campaign as the start of a march to the Indian capital, Delhi. The defeat at Imphal in July destroyed his dreams. In April 1945 Bose escaped to Bangkok, and in May the INA surrendered. In August that year, Bose died in a plane crash in Formosa (Taiwan) on his way to Tokyo.

◀ Members of the Indian National Army celebrate Subhas Chandra Bose's declaration of war on the British and Americans in October 1943.

Calls for independence in India

In India, the Japanese promoted a nationalist group named the Indian Independence League (IIL). The IIL was formed in June 1942. It called on overseas Indians (mostly based in Malaya) to "eliminate the Anglo-Saxons from Asia." These wealthy overseas communities might be able to stir up problems for the British, who then ruled India.

The IIL was led by the charismatic Subhas Chandra Bose. It formed the political base of the Indian National Army (INA). In October 1943, Bose announced the formation of the provisional government of Azad Hind (Free India). Bose would be "netaji," or leader. The Japanese backed Bose's attempt to make his government seem like a real alternative to British colonial rule. They awarded his government the Andaman and Nicobar Islands in the Bay of Bengal.

In early 1944, INA units joined the Japanese invasion of northeastern India from Burma. Bose hoped that the invasion heralded the end of British rule. Instead, Allied victories at the battles of Imphal and Kohima brought northeastern India firmly back under British control.

Eyewitness

❝ Not content with a civil disobedience campaign, Indian people are now morally prepared to employ other means for achieving their liberation. The time has therefore come to pass on to the next stage of our campaign. All organizations, whether inside India or outside, must now transform themselves into a disciplined fighting organization under one leadership. The aim and purpose of this organization should be to take up arms against British imperialism when the time is ripe and signal is given. ❞

Subhas Chandra Bose
June 19, 1942

▶ This Japanese poster was intended to persuade Chinese in Southeast Asia that life would improve under Japanese rule.

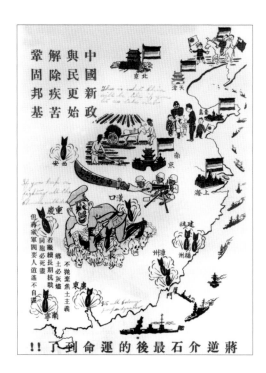

▼ The aftermath of a Japanese air raid on Singapore before the British surrendered. For many of the island's Chinese, Japanese occupation brought further suffering.

Crushing the Singaporean Chinese

The Japanese saw the Indians in Malaya as potentially useful. However, they regarded another large popu-lation group in Malaya as their enemy. This was the overseas Chinese, who were based largely in the island city of Singapore. The overseas Chinese had actively opposed the 1937 Japanese invasion of China. They had raised several million dollars to support the resistance fight on the mainland. Thus, the Japanese saw the Chinese in Singapore as their enemy. When the island's British defenders surrendered on February 15, 1942, Japanese troops set about taking revenge.

The Kempeitai

Within a few days, Singapore City had been placed under the control of the Kempeitai. These military police were Japan's main security and counter-intelligence organization in its occupied territories. The Kempeitai had wide-reaching powers of arrest. It was in

◀ Japanese troops march through Raffles Place, in Singapore, in 1942. In all conquered territories, the government lay either directly or indirectly in the hands of the Japanese military.

charge of destroying all resistance, subversion, and anti-Japanese feeling. The Kempeitai was also responsible for running prison camps and the treatment of POWs. It became notorious for torturing prisoners, and executing them without trial. It also carried out reprisal attacks on civilians suspected of supporting resistance fighters.

Japanese brutality in Singapore

On taking control of Singapore City, the Kempeitai screened every Chinese male between the ages of 15 and 50. It singled out all community leaders, teachers, and known supporters of the China Relief Fund, along with suspected communists. The Kempeitai then took the men to the isolated eastern shore of the island, and executed them. The number killed may have been as high as 10,000. No precise figures exist, and no mass graves have ever been found.

Sex slaves

The Japanese military considered the sexual health of its men to be an essential part of the war effort. They set up military brothels across Asia and the Pacific. The brothels were known as "comfort houses."

The Japanese military police, the Kempeitai, forced women in occupied territories to become what the Japanese called "comfort women." The number of females forced into sex slavery remains unknown; estimates vary from around 30,000 to 100,000. Wherever there were Japanese military bases, from isolated Pacific islands to the Burmese mountains, the Kempeitai ran sex slaves.

About 80 percent of the women who have been identified as sex slaves were Korean. But across the conquered lands, they included women of every Asian nationality. The Kempeitai bullied, threatened, or kidnapped them to work in the sex trade. Some women did not survive the multiple rapes they suffered. The survivors were left physically, emotionally, and psychologically damaged for the rest of their lives.

The Burma Railroad

In October 1942, the Japanese Southern Army began building a 260-mile (415km) single-track railroad from Bangkok, Thailand, to Rangoon, in Burma: the Burma Railroad. The railroad was planned to link Japanese forces in Thailand and Indochina with those in Malaya and the Dutch East Indies. The line was vital to the consolidation of Japanese power. It was due for completion in December 1943. No engineering project on a similar scale had ever been attempted in the region. The route cut through virgin jungle, and across mountains, ravines, rivers, and swamps.

The Japanese did not have much construction equipment or vehicles. What they did have, however, was a huge supply of forced labor. Tens of thousands of Allied prisoners of war built the railroad by hand. They worked in gangs of several hundred. The POWs were led by their own officers but directed by Japanese army engineers. The work was punishing and the treatment brutal. One Japanese officer told prisoners before the work began: "We will build the railroad if we have to build it over the white man's body...."

An estimated 62,000 Allied POWs worked on the railroad. About 30,000 were British, 18,000 Dutch, and 13,000 Australian. There were also about 700 Americans. Up to 300,000 Indian, Malay, and Burmese laborers worked on the project. They were promised wages and decent rations. Instead, they were treated almost as harshly as the prisoners. Hard labor in tropical heat, malnutrition, and diseases such as cholera and malaria killed thousands. In February 1943, the Japanese brought the completion date forward to August. Conditions got even worse. Work went on 24 hours a day through monsoon rains.

The railroad was completed in October 1943. Along its length were the graves of 13,000 Allied prisoners and an estimated 90,000 Asian laborers—a total of 400 dead for every mile of track.

▶ Allied prisoners of war labor in the tropical heat to construct the Burma Railroad, linking Bangkok to Rangoon.

◀ In November 1943, prime minister Tojo summoned Japan's Asian puppet regimes to Tokyo to take part in a congress on the future of the Greater East Asia Co-Prosperity Sphere.

The Japanese campaign of murder moved north to Chinese communities in the southern Malay peninsula. They are thought to have killed a further 20,000 men in Malacca and Seremban. The murders stopped only after Chinese in southern Malaya and Singapore paid Japanese general Yamashita $50 million.

The Japanese called the money an "offering," but it was official Japanese policy to take money from occupied peoples. An organization known as The Total War Institute had helped plan Japan's war. In 1941, it said that conquered peoples had to give up their property or even their lives to pay for their "past mistakes."

An ideal outpost

The Japanese had eliminated what they saw as their main source of opposition in Malaya. They now tried to make Singapore an ideal outpost in the Greater Co-Prosperity Sphere. They renamed the island Syonan (Light of the South) and changed road signs to Japanese. They also set up numerous shrines dedicated to Shinto, which was the Japanese state religion. They set out to promote the Japanese way of life. They renamed the main English-language newspaper *The Syonan Times* and forced schools to teach the Japanese language. Everyone

▼ The tables are turned: Japanese prisoners of war in Singapore clear vegetation from a canal after Japan's surrender in 1945.

▲ A Japanese soldier shares candy with children in the occupied territories of northern China.

in Singapore had to adopt Japanese culture and rituals. The Japanese introduced a new currency, and even altered the time and date. They moved local time two hours head to match Tokyo. Based on the imperial Japanese calendar, 1942 became 2602.

Economic struggles

Despite Japan's ambitious rebranding of Singapore, economic reality soon condemned the Co-Prosperity Sphere to failure. Throughout Southeast Asia, the war had severely affected industry and infrastructure. The Dutch and Indonesians, in particular, had blown up their oil fields before the Japanese could capture them. World trade had collapsed with the onset of global war.

Prison camps

The 1929 Geneva Convention set down rules about the treatment of prisoners of war. Japan signed the convention, but largely ignored it during the war. The only protection prisoners could hope for in

Japanese camps came from the International Red Cross. Japan agreed that the Red Cross could observe prisoners. In December 1941, the Japanese created a POW Information Bureau. However, real control of the camps was in the hands of the Ministry of War and the Kempeitai, the military police. Prisoners had no rights and were used as labor. They were denied any contact with their families. The Japanese treated their prisoners as they wanted. They did not let POWs have mail from home. They also looted their Red Cross parcels, especially for medical supplies.

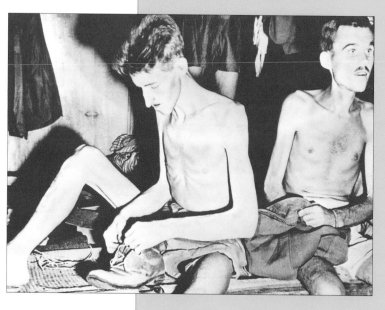

◀ Two malnourished Allied prisoners pack their bags after being freed from a Japanese POW camp in August 1945.

That destroyed the market for commodities such as rubber and tin. The great rubber plantations of Malaya, which the Japanese had made huge efforts to capture, were left to waste.

To make matters worse, the United States launched a campaign of unrestricted submarine warfare. Their submarines sank Japanese merchant vessels in the Pacific on sight. As a result, Japanese imports of raw materials and basic foodstuffs had fallen dramatically by 1944. The Japanese had gone to war largely in order to make sure they had access to supplies of such resources as oil. In 1944, however, only 1.6 million barrels of crude oil reached Japan, compared to 10 million the year before. Imports of rice dropped from 1.4 million tons in 1943 to only 74,000 tons in 1944.

The economy across the region collapsed. Occupation currency of the type the Japanese imposed on Singapore proved to be worthless. By 1943, much of the trade that survived in the region took place through barter, or the exchange of goods for goods. Food essentials—such as rice, sugar, flour, and cooking oil—were in short supply and subject to rationing. Many people died of starvation. Owing to a scarcity of fuel, public utilities also failed. Thousands of people were left homeless and destitute.

A plan for the future

By late 1943, Japan's hold on its Southeast Asian empire was slipping. Allied forces were on the offensive in the Pacific. In November, the Japanese tried to strengthen their control over the Greater Co-Prosperity Sphere.

Resistance groups

Despite Japan's promises of freedom within its Asian Co-Prosperity Sphere, many people responded to the arrival of Japanese troops by organizing armed resistance. This often drew strong support from nationalist groups. They believed that resistance meant freedom not only from the Japanese but also from colonial rule.

▲ Ho Chi Minh was instrumental in leading Vietnam (then part of Indochina) to independence from French colonial rule.

In Malaya, Chinese communists began the Malayan People's Anti-Japanese Army (MPAJA). It ran a guerrilla campaign until 1943, when its leaders were killed. Later that year, the British Special Operations Executive revived the MPAJA by giving it arms and money. In northern Malaya, nationalist Chinese formed the Chinese Anti-Japanese Army in opposition to the MPAJA. The two groups often fought, creating fear among the native Malays. The Malay communists turned on the British after the latter regained control in 1945. This would lead to a long guerrilla war known as the Malay Emergency, which ended in 1960.

In Indochina, a nationalist political party known as the League for the Independence of Vietnam, or Vietminh, was formed in 1941. It fought both French colonial rule and Japanese occupation. Until 1945 it was funded and armed by both America's Office of Strategic Services (OSS) and the Chinese Communist Party. Under the leadership of Ho Chi Minh, the Vietminh then fought against the French, defeating them in 1954. Ho was instrumental in founding the communist state of North Vietnam, which went to war with South Vietnam and the United States in the 1960s.

Civilian captivity

The Japanese imprisoned thousands of civilians living in Asia. They were citizens of both combatant and neutral Western countries. The Japanese invasions of December 1941 were so quick that civilians had no time to flee. For example, some 14,000 U.S. civilians fell into Japanese hands. Some historians argue that their capture could have been avoided. Both the U.S. and British governments knew that a Japanese attack in Southeast Asia was increasingly likely. Both could have had time to begin to evacuate their citizens from areas of potential danger.

The Japanese regarded Western civilians as unwelcome colonists in Asia. They treated them badly. They refused to repatriate or exchange them for Japanese civilians, such as those interned by the British in India. Instead, they kept them in camps in conditions little better than those of prisoners of war.

One of the most infamous camps, Changi, on Singapore's eastern coast, held both civilians and prisoners of war. The Japanese kept soldiers and civilians, and men and women, in separate compounds. In March 1942 there were just under 2,600 civilians in Changi, including more than 400 women and children. The total had grown to 3,460 by September 1943.

At first, many prisoners attempted to maintain some semblance of their previous lives. They formed social clubs and published newsletters; some even tried to maintain the class structures typical of colonial European society. But as their captivity lengthened from months into years, and hardship, disease, and shortage of food took their toll, life in the civilian camps increasingly became a fight for survival.

◀ An American and a Dutch woman do their daily chores in a Japanese internment camp on the island of Singapore.

They held a Greater East Asia Congress in Tokyo. They summoned representatives from their puppet regimes in Manchuria, the Philippines, and Burma. They also invited observers from Thailand and Bose's Free India movement. Prime Minister Tojo told delegates that Burma and the Philippines would have self-government. Their economic and foreign affairs were to remain in Japanese hands, however. Singapore and Malaya, together with Java and Sumatra in the Dutch East Indies, would become colonies ruled directly from Tokyo. Korea and Formosa (Taiwan) were

See Also
● The defeat of the British and Dutch, p.28
● The fall of the Philippines, p.42
● The U.S. submarine campaign, Vol.6, p.48
● Axis Home Fronts, Vol.7, p.36

◄ Filipino guerrilla fighters, escorted by a pack mule, take position with machine guns and rifles stolen from the Japanese.

already governed in that way. These new colonies produced rubber and oil. They were the most important resources for Japan's war effort. Thailand would become a protectorate. In theory it was independent, but it was actually under Japanese control.

The beginning of the end

The Greater East Asia Congress was Japan's last attempt to impose a territorial settlement on its conquests in Asia. The Congress made its final declaration on November 6, 1943. It declared that Japan's aim was to build a Greater East Asia based on the principles of "common prosperity and well-being based on justice." A second congress was planned for 1944, but it never took place. Within seven months of the declaration, the first U.S. B-29s were flying bombing raids over southern Japan. Within a year, the Japanese fleet in the Pacific had been broken at the Battle of Leyte Gulf.

▼ Native laborers work in a smithy during the building of a railroad in Burma.

TIMELINE

1939

SEPTEMBER: German troops invade and overrun Poland; Britain and France declare war on Germany; the Soviet Union invades eastern Poland and extends control to the Baltic states. The Battle of the Atlantic begins.

NOVEMBER: The Soviet Union launches a winter offensive against Finland.

1940

APRIL: Germany invades Denmark and Norway; British attack German shipping off Narvik and Bergen; Allied troops land in Norway.

MAY: Germany invades Luxembourg, the Netherlands, Belgium, and France; Allied troops are evacuated at Dunkirk.

JUNE: Allied troops withdraw from Norway; Italy declares war on France and Britain; German troops enter Paris; France signs an armistice with Germany; Italy bombs Malta in the Mediterranean.

JULY: German U-boats inflict heavy losses on Allied convoys in the Atlantic; Britain sends warships to neutralize the French fleet at Mers el-Kébir, in Algeria, North Africa; German raids on shipping and ports in the English Channel open the Battle of Britain.

SEPTEMBER: Luftwaffe air raids begin the Blitz— the bombing of London and other British cities; Italian troops advance from Libya into Egypt; Germany, Italy, and Japan sign the Tripartite Pact.

OCTOBER: Italy invades Greece; the British navy attacks the Italian fleet at Taranto; Greek forces, aided by the British, mount a counterattack against the Italians.

DECEMBER: British troops rout the Italians at Sidi Barrani, Egypt.

1941

JANUARY: Allied units capture Tobruk in Libya; British forces in Sudan attack Italian East Africa.

FEBRUARY: Allies defeat Italy at Benghazi, Libya; Rommel's Afrika Korps arrive in Tripoli.

MARCH: The Africa Korps drive British troops back from El Agheila; the Italian fleet is defeated by the British at the Battle of Matapan.

APRIL: German, Italian, and Hungarian units invade Yugoslavia; German forces invade Greece; the Afrika Korps beseige Tobruk.

MAY: German battleship *Bismarck* sinks HMS *Hood*, but is sunk by the British fleet a few days later.

JUNE: German troops invade the Soviet Union

JULY: German forces advance to within 10 miles (16km) of Kiev.

AUGUST: The United States bans the export of oil to Japan.

SEPTEMBER: German forces start the siege of Leningrad; German Army Group Center mounts a campaign to attack Moscow.

NOVEMBER: British troops begin an attack to relieve Tobruk; the Allies liberate Ethiopia.

DECEMBER: Japanese aircraft attack the U.S. Pacific Fleet at Pearl Harbor; Japan declares war on the United States and Britain; the United States, Britain, and the Free French declare war on Japan; Japanese forces invade the Philippines, Malaya, and Thailand, and defeat the British garrison in Hong Kong.

1942

JANUARY: Japan attacks the Dutch East Indies and invades Burma; Rommel launches a new offensive in Libya; Allied troops withdraw from Malaya.

FEBRUARY: Singapore surrenders to the Japanese.

APRIL: The Bataan Peninsula in the Philippines falls to the Japanese, as does Mandalay in Burma.

MAY: U.S. and Japanese fleets clash at the Battle of the Coral Sea; Rommel attacks the Gazala Line in Libya; British RAF launches a major bombing raid against Cologne.

JUNE: The U.S. Navy defeats the Japanese at the Battle of Midway; Rommel recaptures Tobruk and the Allies retreat to Egypt.

JULY: The Germans take Sebastopol after a long siege; they advance into the Caucasus.

AUGUST: U.S. Marines encounter fierce Japanese resistance in the Solomons.

SEPTEMBER–OCTOBER: Allied forces defeat Axis troops at El Alamein, Egypt—the first major Allied victory of the war.

NOVEMBER: Three Allied task forces land U.S. and British troops in Morocco and Algeria.

1943

FEBRUARY: The German Sixth Army surrenders at Stalingrad; the Japanese evacuate troops from Guadalcanal in the Solomons; the Chindits conduct their first mission in Burma.

MAY: Axis forces in Tunisia surrender, marking the end of the campaign in North Africa.

JULY: U.S. troops make landings on New Georgia Island in the Solomons; the Red Army wins the Battle of Kursk; Allied troops land on Sicily; British bombers conduct massive raids on Hamburg.

AUGUST: German forces occupy Italy; the Soviets retake Kharkov.

SEPTEMBER: Allied units begin landings on mainland Italy; Italy surrenders, prompting a German invasion of northern Italy.

OCTOBER: The Red Army completes the liberation of the Caucasus.

NOVEMBER: U.S. carrier aircraft attack Rabaul in the Solomons.

1944

JANUARY: The German siege of Leningrad ends.

FEBRUARY: U.S. forces complete their conquest of the Marshall Islands.

MARCH: The Soviet offensive reaches the Dniester River; Allied aircraft bomb the monastery at Monte Cassino in Italy.

JUNE: U.S. troops enter the city of Rome; D-Day–the Allies begin the invasion of northern Europe; U.S. aircraft defeat the Japanese fleet at the Battle of the Philippine Sea.

JULY: The Red Army begins its offensive to clear the Baltic states; Soviet tanks enter Poland.

AUGUST: Japanese troops withdraw from Myitkyina in Burma; French forces liberate Paris; Allied units liberate towns in France, Belgium, and the Netherlands.

OCTOBER: Soviet and Yugoslavian troops capture Belgrade, the Yugoslav capital; the Japanese suffer defeat at the Battle of Leyte Gulf.

DECEMBER: Hitler counterattacks in the Ardennes in the Battle of the Bulge.

1945

JANUARY: The U.S. Army makes an unopposed landing on Luzon in the Philippines; the Red Army liberates Auschwitz; most of Poland and Czechoslovakia are liberated by the Allies.

FEBRUARY: U.S. troops take the Philippine capital, Manila, and land on the island of Iwo Jima; Soviet troops strike west across Germany; the U.S. Army heads toward the Rhine River.

APRIL: U.S. troops land on the island of Okinawa; Mussolini is shot by partisans; Soviet troops assault Berlin; Hitler commits suicide in his bunker.

MAY: All active German forces surrender.

JUNE: Japanese resistance ends in Burma and on Okinawa.

AUGUST: Atomic bombs are dropped on Hiroshima and Nagasaki; Japan surrenders; Soviet troops in Manchuria defeat the Kwantung Army.

GLOSSARY

advance A general move forward by a military force.

Allies One of the two groups of combatants in the war. The main Allies were Britain, the Soviet Union, the United States, British Empire troops, and free forces from occupied nations.

amphibious assault A landing from the sea, usually by infantry and artillery supported by naval and air power.

area bombing A form of aerial bombing aimed at a whole area rather than a specific target within it.

armistice A temporary halt in fighting agreed to by both sides.

armor A term referring to armored vehicles, such as tanks.

army group Two or more armies grouped together.

artillery Large weapons such as big guns and howitzers.

Axis One of the two groups of combatants in the war. The leading Axis powers were Germany, Italy, and Japan.

blitzkrieg A German word meaning "lightning war." It referred to the tactic of rapid land advance supported by great airpower.

bridgehead A small advanced position captured in enemy territory.

casualty Someone who is killed or wounded in conflict, or who is missing but probably dead.

corps An army formation smaller than an army, made up of a number of divisions operating together under a general.

counteroffensive A set of attacks that defend against enemy attacks.

dive-bomber A war plane that dives toward its target before releasing its bombs at low altitude.

diversion A dummy exercise intended to draw the enemy away from a real attack.

empire A group of a number of countries governed by a single country.

embargo An order to temporarily stop something, especially trading

evacuation The act of moving someone from danger to a safe position.

garrison A group of troops placed to defend a location.

Holocaust The systematic German campaign to exterminate millions of Jews and others.

independence The state of self-government for a people or nation.

infantry soldiers who are trained to fight on foot, or in vehicles.

kamikaze Japanese for "divine wind"; the name refers to Japan's suicide pilots.

landing craft Shallow-bottomed boats designed to carry troops and supplies from ships to the shore.

mandate An authorization to perform to govern a territory; a mandated territory.

Marine A soldier who serves in close association with naval forces.

occupation The seizure and control of an area by military force.

offensive A planned military attack.

rationing A system of limiting food and other supplies to ensure that everyone gets a similar amount.

reconnaissance A small-scale survey of enemy territory to gather information.

resources Natural materials that are the basis of economic wealth, such as oil, rubber, and agricultural produce.

strategy A detailed plan for achieving success.

strongpoint Any defensive position that has been strengthened to withstand an attack.

sortie A mission flown by a single plane.

siege A military blockade of a place, such as a city, to force it to surrender.

troops Groups of soldiers

FURTHER READING

BOOKS

General

Lewis, Jon E. *The Mammoth Book of Eyewitness World War II.* New York: Carroll and Graf Publishers, 2002.

Mullener, Elizabeth. *War Stories: Remembering World War II.* Baton Rouge, LA: Louisiana State University Press, 2004.

Shaw, Antony. *World War II Day by Day.* Osceola, WI: MBI Publishing Co, 2000.

Story, Ronald. *Concise Historical Atlas of World War II: The Geography of Conflict.* New York: Oxford University Press, 2005.

Willmott, H.P., Robin Cross, and Charles Messenger. *World War II.* New York: Dorling Kindersley, 2004.

World War II (3 volumes). Tarrytown, NY: Marshall Cavendish Corporation, 2003.

Western Front

Ambrose, Stephen E. *Citizen Soldiers: The U.S. Army from the Normandy Beaches to the Bulge to the Surrender of Germany.* New York: Simon and Schuster, 1998.

Hall, Anthony. *D-Day: Operation Overlord Day by Day.* US: Osceola, WI: MBI Publishing Co., 2003.

Hastings, Max: *Armageddon: The Battle for Germany, 1944–1945.* New York: A.A. Knopf, 2004.

Eastern Front

Beevor, Antony. *Stalingrad.* New York: Viking, 1998.

Beevor, Antony. *Berlin: The Downfall, 1945.* New York: Viking, 2002.

Crawford, Steve. *The Eastern Front Day by Day, 1941–45: A Photographic Chronology.* Dulles, VA: Potomac Books, 2006.

Overy, Richard. *Russia's War.* New York: TV Books, 1997.

Pacific War

Davison, John. *Pacific War Day by Day.* Osceola, WI: MBI Publishing Co., 2006.

Stein, R. Conrad. *World War 2 in the Pacific (American War Series).* Berkeley Heights, NJ: Enslow Publishers, 2002.

Aftermath

Gaddis, John Lewis. *The Cold War: A New History.* New York: Penguin Press, 2005.

Judt, Toby. *Postwar: A History of Europe Since 1945.* New York: Penguin Press, 2005.

WEB SITES

www.bbc.co.uk/history/war/wwtwo/
BBC History Web site, World War II index page

www.spartacus.schoolnet.co.uk/2WW.htm
Index to resources on World War II.

www.historyplace.com/worldwar2/timeline/ww2time.htm
The History Place World War II timeline, with many links

www.grolier.com/wwii/wwii_mainpage.html
Comprehensive Grolier commemoration of World War II

www.yale.edu/lawweb/avalon/wwii/wwii
The Avalon Project: primary sources for important war documents and speeches

DVD/Video

The World at War (30th Anniversary Edition) (5 discs). A&E Home Video, 2004.

The Nazis: A Warning from History (2 discs). BBC Warner, 2005.

BBC History of World War II (12 discs). BBC Warner, 2005.

INDEX

PICTURE CREDITS

Front Cover: Lebrecht Collection
Title Page: Robert Hunt Library

Corbis: 41b, 57t, 57b, 63b, Bettmann 53t, Hulton Deutsch Collection 11, Underwood & Underwood 9bl; **Getty Images:** 7, 26t, 41t, 56, 60t, 60b, 64t, 67b; **Lebrecht Collection:** 20, 22; **National Archives:** 27, 51b; **Robert Hunt Library:** 6, 8, 9tr 10t, 10b, 12t, 13, 14, 15, 16/17, 19t, 19b, 23t, 23b, 24, 26b, 28/29, 30, 31, 32, 33t, 33b, 34t, 34b, 35, 36, 37, 38, 39t, 39b, 40, 42/43, 44t, 44b, 46t, 46b, 47, 49t, 49b, 50, 51t, 52, 53b, 59, 63t, 64b, 66; **Topfoto:** 4/5, 18, 25, 54/55, 58t, 58b, 61, 62, 67t, Abin-Guillot Roger Viollet 65, Roger Viollet 12b.